Training Children
for
Maturity

TRAINING CHILDREN
FOR
MATURITY

by
Louis Evely

Translated by
Edmond Bonin

NEWMAN PRESS
Westminster, Md.   New York, N. Y.   Glen Rock, N. J.
Amsterdam   Toronto

This book is a translation of *Eduquer en s'Eduquant* and the essay *Liberté* by Louis Evely.

NIHIL OBSTAT:
Donald J. Gervais, S.T.D., J.C.L.
Censor Deputatus

IMPRIMATUR:
✠ Bernard J. Flanagan, D.D.
Bishop of Worcester

August 7, 1967

The Nihil Obstat and Imprimatur are official declarations that a book or pamphlet is free of doctrinal or moral error. No implication is contained therein that those who have granted the Nihil Obstat and Imprimatur agree with the contents, opinions or statements expressed.

Library of Congress
Catalog Card Number: 68-16675

Jacket Design: Morris Berman

Published by Newman Press
Editorial Office: 304 W. 58th St., N.Y., N.Y. 10019
Business Office: Glen Rock, New Jersey 07452

Printed and bound in the
United States of America
by The Colonial Press Inc.,
Clinton, Mass.

Contents

PART II

At School

APPENDIX

Freedom

Part I
AT HOME

I
Child Training and Modern Psychology

Progress in the physical sciences has unduly distracted modern man from his primary field of knowledge and activity: himself. Though impressively learned in all other spheres, he has increasingly become for himself "the unknown" about whom Alexis Carrel wrote. Fortunately, contemporary psychology, heeding the age-old wisdom of "Know thyself," has begun to regain lost ground and prove triumphantly that there is more to discover in human nature than anywhere else. Our soul holds secrets infinitely more stupendous than those of neutrons and protons. So far, we have colonized only a narrow coastal strip of it; we have scratched the surface, but we do not suspect the minable riches in its extraordinarily deep and fecund substratum. Just as today's scientists have prodigiously outstripped the intuitions of medieval alchemists, magicians and astrologers, so our psychologists are systematically exploring the depths of the soul where mediums, fakirs and yogis once penetrated only by accident or effraction.

This inquiry is not over, but the results of it have already revolutionized our views on man and, consequently, on his upbringing; amid many humiliating and disquieting revelations, new possibilities keep opening up to us. Since the middle of the sixteenth century we have been handed four particularly severe but, in a way, liberative humiliations. The first came from Copernicus, who demonstrated that the sun does not rotate around the earth and that we are not the center of the universe. The second came from Darwin, who asserted that man is descended from animals. The third from Marx, who taught that, in the history of humanity, the im-

3

portance of economic facts singularly limits that of men and ideas. And the fourth from Freud, who gave the deathblow to our pride by bringing to light the influence of our instincts and our unconscious. Psychological phenomena, he pointed out, need not be conscious in order to be efficacious: we can be swayed by motives that escape us. Accordingly, we sometimes do right for the wrong reason and always have a good one to do evil. Not endowed with freedom, we have to attain it by broadening our range of consciousness.

This new knowledge helps us to treat the mentally ill, who perhaps outnumber the physically ill. Like the gamut from colds to leprosy, there is a vast spectrum of moral infirmities, of psychological mutilations. Millions of unfortunates in apparently good health have not reached affective, social or sexual maturity. But, above all, these discoveries should serve to prevent illness. When, for example, we consider the high percentage of college and university dropouts, we cannot but question the adequacy of the moral and intellectual equipment given them to face these ordeals.

The Critical Age

The first point psychologists emphasize is the crucial importance of the events that occur during infancy. Neuroses in adults stem from shocks sustained usually during the first six years of life. When borne unsatisfactorily, all such experiences, though repressed, remain operative, weighing upon and warping personality. Most of us are unaware of the enormous difficulties which the very young child encounters and must overcome; and if we knew, we would not care to start life over again. Take the ordeal of birth. It must be exactly like death: being expelled from a happy, passive state to which we were perfectly adapted and in which all our functions were carried out most conveniently and satisfactorily, and being precipitated into a cold, harsh and strange world where we need all our stamina to survive. Which of us could face this confidently? We should hardly be surprised, then, if infants, with their primitive mental processes, react to such a shock with fear, fury, revolt and a desperate search for that maternal shelter, that lost paradise for which they feel an overpowering and lifelong nostalgia. And we are not born only once: weaning, puberty, adolescence and death itself are progressive births. Throughout life we learn to accept being born; throughout life we are torn by a twofold pull: the promise of the future, with an urge to exercise our new powers and our love of independence, and, on the other hand, a longing for the past, with the memory of the sure pleasures of passivity and the desire to retreat into an utterly unconscious and parasitic state. All the medical safeguards that surround mother and child at birth prompt us to ask how we can help the little one psychologically as well. In this connection, modern psychology has discovered that scientific child-rearing centers inspired by purely hygienic theories are worthless. What an infant needs most at birth is to find affection and attach himself to someone whom he can love and recognize.

But further difficulties lie ahead—for example, the birth of a new baby. Try to imagine how a child feels when, after having been the center of the family, his mother's pride and the object of everyone's assiduous coddling, he hears talk of a possible rival: "Mother's going to have another little one soon!" Some parents unthinkingly use this as a threat when their child misbehaves. Even if they do not, the first act by which the newborn manifests his existence is to take the mother away from home and make her disappear for several days. When she returns, she is completely engrossed in her baby, whose demands on her love and time strike the older child as an injustice against him. Every addition to the family repeats the story of Esau and Jacob, and many a mother plays Rebekah. It is not surprising, then, that the elder feels sad, jealous and resentful. If he dares give vent to his perfectly natural spite, matters get worse: he is blamed and punished and less loved for it. No wonder he fails to understand the situation, begins to hate his rival secretly, and decides to regain his mother's love by acting like a baby again, wetting the bed, whining and calling attention to himself by sheer disagreeableness. The ideal which the family tacitly inculcates in him is regression, not growth. If, on the contrary, his parents prepare him for this new situation, he will find in it an opportunity for development. They should let his jealousy express itself, helping him understand it and doing everything to dispel it, and orient him to a new conception of his place in the family, asking him to perform little services, confiding that they hope their newborn will become like him someday, complimenting him oftener than before on his behavior and his cleverness, but above all continuing to show him a great deal of attention and love.

Even the simplest and most placid existence affords occasions for traumatism in the child. One such circumstance is his first punishment. He clings to his mother closer than to anyone else on earth; but when she punishes him, he feels that she is deliberately withholding her affection and depriving him of her presence. To the fury that flames up in him there is added the fear of being separated from her still longer if he persists in his rebellion. He simply does not understand that she is acting through love and for his own good. Thus, his world falls apart and he is thrown into a cruel and terrifying universe where nothing is sure and anything can happen, where he can be hurt at any moment and suddenly robbed of what he needs most. Love, hate and fear—what will emerge from the conflict between these three exacerbated emotions? A mother's tact can attenuate these crises, but no one can boast of obviating them altogether.

Aggressiveness

Such observations have highlighted the importance of aggressiveness, that vital quality which enables us to face danger, surmount obstacles and learn to accept failure. Beware of overdocile children: they lack spirit. "He's so nice, so polite," mothers will rhapsodize, "as sweet as a girl. He's so tenderhearted he can't bear to hurt me!" Yet, eventually, a boy must be strong enough to cross others, inflict pain and achieve independence; he will have to resist imploring voices, tear-filled eyes and tender reproaches. Where will he find the courage he needs? Did he ever truly obey if he was incapable of disobeying? Did he practice the evangelical counsel of meekness if he was afraid of violence? The normal child is one whose fortitude preserves him from both excessive docility and excessive tenacity. (For tenacity, also, is symptomatic of anxiety and weakness. It takes courage to change one's mind—and especially one's character and conduct.)

Two opposite causes rob children of aggressiveness: too much pampering and too much repression. The pampered have never grappled with difficulties because everything has been done for them and nothing required of them. A spoiled child is not one for whom we have done too much (we can never do too much for a child), but one from whom we have exacted nothing in return, one whom we have not taught to give according as he has received. He will be unable to endure frustration and defeat.

Pavlov's disciples have succeeded in showing the results of such training even in monkeys. Ten monkeys are lined up along one wall of a room, and against the opposite wall there stands a large chest of drawers filled with bananas. At the sound of a siren, the monkeys are let loose. They soon discover the drawers, pull them open, and devour the bananas. This procedure is repeated until the monkeys automatically run to the chest the instant they hear the signal. For them, siren, drawers and bananas are one and the same thing. After a "vacation," the conditioned subjects are led back into the same room. Suddenly the siren shrieks. They dash forth, yank the drawers open—and find them empty. Most of the monkeys then exhibit the outward signs of a definite nervous breakdown: they beat their breasts and slump to the floor in a neurasthenic lethargy.

Many a child who is accustomed to finding the refrigerator always well-stocked, and many a grown-up who has never lacked anything, shows the same symptoms as those monkeys the first time he is disappointed.

But the contrary method produces the same results. A child who has been treated too severely, punished excessively, forbidden to do anything, and given no freedom or room for initiative, is just as unprepared for life as a mollycoddle. Overexacting fathers are no better than overindulgent mothers.

Love and Firmness

Children need love and firmness alike.

Love is creative; only the insane generosity of love could beget life. Picture two adults, two full-blown personalities leaning with total devotion over a little baby, passionately subordinating themselves to him, setting infinite value on him, ready to sacrifice their possessions and their very life for this insignificant and unknown being who as yet just barely exists. Thanks to their prodigality, he comes into this world, survives, smiles, finds the normal conditions for his development and, one day, awakens to the love that created him.

When he reaches fifteen or sixteen, however, his parents are often bewildered because he no longer resembles the child they have loved. Frequently, too, this is the age when they think they know him and can judge him. To tell the truth, it is the age when they do not love him any more and, consequently, cease creating him. For loving someone means believing and having confidence in him forever.

Parents who stop believing in their child's unlimited potential for good stop loving him. Since they no longer have enough faith and courage to love him, he turns to outsiders and looks around for a friend, a teacher, anyone who can believe in him again and thereby enable him to grow.

He will grow only for those who love him. What he will most appreciate is the way their loving faith so heartens him that he actually dares to be much better with them, much tenderer, much more vulnerable and generous than he could ever be with anyone else.

Until he has been loved this way, he will remain dormant, with no rights or place of his own in this world, and no interest in life. If he is to accept and love others, he must first be accepted and loved and thus taught to accept and love himself. Egoists may appear self-seeking, but that is because they have not found themselves; they may act as if they "own the place," but that is often because they feel out of place. On the other hand, when a child has been loved, wholeheartedly accepted, understood, protected and thus shown his infinite worth, he can become a secure and high-minded adult who, throughout life, will unflaggingly and confidently strive to rebuild this lost paradise. "Everyone who has had a real childhood," says Etienne De Greef, "is a fallen god who remembers heaven."

But, along with love, a child requires authority. Firmness in his parents is just as indispensable to his feeling of security as is their affection. He appreciates the support of unflinching authority, which both reassures and stimulates him. Small as he may be, he revels in activity and danger, and objects if we try to help too much: "Joe big enough, Joe do it!" At the same time, he loves order and, as Maria Montessori observed, feels such a vital need for it that, when he plays, he always hides in the same few places and protests if we pretend to be looking for him elsewhere. For him, the best thing in the world is the order in it, the faithfulness and the familiarity of it: with his eyes closed, he can lay hands on what he desires. This is the age when we implant those solid habits which will always prove helpful because they put order in his life.

You may complain that "Be neither harsh nor weak" is easier said than done. Of course it is, but no one ever seriously thought that being a parent was easy. Children have to be loved and kept under control; they have to receive and give; they have to absorb so much love that they can offer it to others someday.

Would you rather be loved by someone whom you do not care for, or love someone who does not care for you? That is the acid test of maturity. No doubt you dream of loving someone who loves you also; but that is too beautiful and rarely happens—at least not simultaneously—and you should not base your life on such utopian expectations. One friend or one spouse almost invariably trails behind the other. (We can only hope it is not always the same one.)

For all of us the crucial question is this: What makes us feel happier and richer—being loved and surrounded with attention, or being able to love and go out to others? In one of his novels, Georges Duhamel shows the Pasquier family gathered around

Cécile, the artist, the inspired one, who is playing piano for them. Hardly has she begun when each automatically returns to his favorite dreams and isolates himself once again in his private world of thought. The father recalls the women he has known, the mother broods over her children and her anxieties, one daughter meditates on the baby she is expecting, and so on. But Justin thinks of Cécile and his hopeless love for her. Realizing that she could never love him, an insignificant and unprepossessing Jew, he sits there tormenting himself. Gradually, however, under the spell of her music, all these ruminations change and soar high above the earth; something luminous transforms them, and Justin thinks, "How I love Cécile! What a joy, what a blessing to know and love her! I'm all the richer for this experience, but she's poor because she hasn't tasted this love. Never can I be grateful enough to her. I love her; I have something to give her and, perhaps, teach her. I'd want her to be as rich as I am in my heart of hearts!" At that moment, he crossed over from childhood into maturity.

Childhood is preeminently the period of egoism and self-seeking. A baby considers himself the center of the universe: everything in it exists only to serve him. All he does is demand, grasp, absorb, fling aside and scream with rage or sorrow if contradicted. All he knows is how to take, receive, and be loved. An adult, on the contrary, is—or should be—someone who has learned to love, to give, to devote himself and be so happy about it that he desires nothing in return. Modern psychology, though much maligned, nevertheless takes a profoundly Christian view of man: it teaches that his entire development consists in passing from infantile selfishness to adult generosity, from the need of receiving love to the capacity for giving it.

Sexuality

This passage from selfishness to generosity is the meaning which modern psychologists attach to the notion of sexuality, a word that has sufficed to make some condemn and others extol the theories of Freud. He recognized the patent fact that sexuality exists in children and thereby shocked all those who believe that silence eliminates problems, who feel that sex is too base ever to think about (whereas they should think about it in order to humanize it), and who like to idealize childhood purity as if there were no such thing as adult purity (which is infinitely more precious and which they should acquire instead of growing lyrical over the virtue they imagine they once had and then lost—conveniently—forever).

Every mother has noticed that her little girls strike poses in the presence of men, and that her little boys smile more readily at women. This attraction toward the opposite sex exists from earliest childhood; and, rather than snicker about it among ourselves idiotically, we should teach children love and renunciation, and rely on this magnetic force to help them transcend themselves.

The Oedipus Complex

Boys need their mother's love, and girls have to feel that their father is interested in them. This initial success, the assurance that they can create interest and inspire affection, is indispensable if children are to develop. As I said earlier, we grow only for those who love us: there is no use being beautiful, strong, intelligent and noble except for someone by whom we are cherished. A little girl whose father sends her back to her dolls because he is interested only in his sons or his business discourages her from growing and—what is worse—from accepting her sex. She concludes, "If I can't make anyone care for me, what's the use of being a girl?" One tot complained comically, "All the men I like are already taken: Daddy has Mommy, and God has the Blessed Virgin." That line is good for more than laughs. A young girl has a serious problem when she does not know what to do in life and cannot see whom it is worthwhile growing up for. Many a woman has never been able to accept her nature and wishes she were a man—that carefree, independent, sensual, selfish creature whom she has been reduced to envying because, as a child, she was not sufficiently encouraged to find her happiness in spreading joy and beauty, smiling and bringing others to smile, loving and awakening love in their hearts. Only then is it worth being a woman.

In the same way, too many mothers rejoice if their son works industriously and shows no interest in the opposite sex. This is a rather shortsighted ideal. Developing a child's affective life is just as important as molding his will and his intellect, and even more delicate. Principally the mother's task, it obliges her to keep asking, "Is my child becoming capable of genuine love? Whom does he love? How and when does he manifest the goodness of his heart?" The first person he learns to love is his mother, and everything depends on that first experience, that first love. Mother and son are bound by extraordinarily strong emotional ties which every true mother senses with a mixture of dread and delight.

(She is apprehensive—or should be—for she realizes that she can maim and even kill his affective powers, or so monopolize and attach him to herself that he cannot go out to others, either male or female, but is virtually castrated and turned into her plaything, her possession. No one can deny that Mauriac's Genitrix could and does exist; we have all met her, and every woman at some time or other finds herself acting like her.)

But this understanding, this vital communication between a mother and her children allows them to receive from her everything that she wants and is able to give them. She can fill them with tenderness and pride, with assurance and nobility; she, and she alone, can teach them to admire and love their father. In fact, the unique way she loves him is what will rub off on the children. For boys are instinctively jealous of their father, as anyone with half an eye can observe; but, at the same time, they admire him and need to have their mother love him and hold him up as an ideal, while her love encourages them to hope that they can someday become like him. She must bring them forth into the world of men a second time by restoring them to their father. There, it becomes his duty to welcome and guide them.

The Superiority Complex

Let the father take care not to crush his children under the weight of his dignity and his adult exigencies; but, remembering and comparing his experiences with theirs, let him assure them that they can resemble him sooner or later, since, at their age, he himself was no better than they are now.

The average father treats his sons with gross injustice. From a distance of thirty years, he makes depressing comparisons and then waxes indignant because the disheartened boys fail to improve. They would do wonders if he sat down with them and admitted, in all simplicity and sincerity, "When I was your age, I made the same mistakes you do. I wasn't interested in hard work, either. And I just couldn't confide in my father. But here's how I learned; here's what made me change. . . . You're already better than I was at your age: you do this and that far better than I did. Later on, you'll be way ahead of me." A heart-to-heart talk like this fills boys with humility and enthusiasm. They discover that Dad is "a great guy" and feel that they are not doing enough to show their love and follow in his footsteps, but that, with his advice and help, they may eventually succeed in doing so. Then, conscious of all the love that has brought them into being, they can enter into a joyous emulation of their friends, their father and other men.

I imagine there is not a single well-born boy who, at some time, has not wanted to become like his father, but I have practically never met one who would admit it. Repeated failure, censorious teachers and perhaps their own father so thoroughly persuade these boys they can never rise to his level that they stop trying. When questioned about their plans for the future, they answer in terms that mean "I want to do anything except what my father does." Then I remember a text from Saint John: "The Son can do nothing by himself; he can do only what he sees the Father doing. . . . For the Father loves the Son and shows him everything he does himself . . . and whatever the Father does the Son does too."

Too few fathers have the patience and the humility to "show" themselves like that. Too many are bigwigs to their employees, their clients and their secretary; but to their son, they are distant, mysterious, overworked, nervous and inaccessible strangers. Most boys, in spite of their deep-rooted aspiration to become like their father, cannot form a clear picture of him, his work or his character. For all practical purposes, he is away from home so often that masculine values hardly seem cogent there, and the only ideal presented is feminine values, which are very annoying but ensnaring for a boy. Family life should be organized in such a way that the sons, before they are asked to become men, see the desirability of doing so. In many homes there is only one concrete ideal—the mother. For that reason, it is imperative that she serve as an intermediary and lead her boys to the knowledge and love of their father.

So, too, with the girls. Their father's profound affection, which makes them accept their femininity, should also give them back to their mother and introduce them to the female world, making them desire and hope to become like other women. For a long time, they have been prepared for this by the courtesies and compliments he has paid them and their mother, as well as by the services and the qualities he has elicited from them.

But their mother must welcome them into her world. Here again, lack of sincerity, warmth and trust breeds incomprehension. "To love," says Gabriel Marcel, "is to have confidence in someone forever." Instead of growing indignant over her daughters' stupidities and blunders, she would do well to tell them of her own. Girls come to us priests for advice on flirtations, mistakes and imprudences which are not half so dangerous as the secrecy that surrounds them. If we ask, "Why don't you discuss this with your mother?" we are always told, "Oh, she'd never understand such things! She's too rigid. Mother has never loved anybody but Dad; she hasn't had any experience. . . ." A mother's first duty is to persuade her daughters that they have everything they need in order to become better than she.

Sexual Development

Man is sexed because God is triune. This statement will shock many, but many need to be shocked into thinking. After stating that God made man in his own image and likeness, the Book of Genesis quietly adds: "In the image of God he created him, male and female he created them." Man and woman—that means "capable of loving."

God is love. He is not solitary, selfish or "celibate," as Chateaubriand would have him. The Preface of the Blessed Trinity sings, "Not in the oneness of a single person," which is like saying, "How wonderful that you are not alone, but that you are several, that you are Love!" In God, they had to be several in order to be God; they had to be several in order to be Love.

Having been created in the likeness of God, man always needs someone else in order to be himself. Without her husband, a wife feels uncertain, paralyzed, incomplete; so also a husband without his wife, and children who have lost their parents. What is best and most divine in man is this inability to be completely self-sufficient or withdraw wholly into himself. Hell is the tranquil possession of self, whereas heaven is total availability to others. So many people confuse both.

God could have designed humans to reproduce by scissiparity or parthenogenesis. But then we would be solitary and dispensed from loving. (What ideal purity for all the proponents of negative morality!) And we would not be created in his image. We would not feel this powerful urge to give ourselves which makes our body capable of ministering and reverberating with the aspirations of our mind and heart.

Moreover, the importance of sexuality far transcends the couple and reproduction. The whole life of society, the entire network of human relationships depends on this ability to unite, to interest ourselves in others, to complement and be complemented by our fellowman. Original sin crippled our capacity to love. Its consequences, then, are social much more than individual. When

we mention original sin, everyone starts scrutinizing his own concupiscence for traces of it. Yet original sin consists above all in the
fact that we do not and cannot love. And concupiscence is like a
dying ember, covered with ashes, which no longer throws light or
heat but can still burn the unwary.

The whole result of training and grace should be to revive our
ability to love. To that end, man undergoes a long evolution. As
a child, he is self-centered and enslaved to his appetites, so that all
he can do is demand and receive. He may remain at this stage
throughout life; but if he grows, instead, puberty offers him a chance
to break free. For at that difficult and dangerous age, which many
educators equate with sins of impurity, there appear the first weak
stirrings of love. A child has only playmates, but an adolescent
discovers friends and learns that there are people on whom he can
lavish more attention, admiration and love than on himself. Locked
inside his ego, he could never know and love humanity, for then
it seemed a ponderous and worrisome burden imposed on him
from without. But now that he reaches out to others, he sights a
boundless new world and loves himself better in loving his neighbor. How beautiful are those who teach him the grandeur of man
and the meaning of human life!

Still, he is reluctant to emerge from his carapace and risk his
neck. Love is frightening: it makes him vulnerable and puts him
at someone else's mercy. An adolescent's spontaneous ideal is self-
defense: to go through life impassible and unassailable, secure and
well protected—or should I say: preserved from loving, but
capable of seducing? Then, he meets someone who is warm and
sensitive and vibrant and young, someone who walks about defenseless among all the shapes which are trembling with fear
inside their suits of armor. That day, he discovers where true nobility and courage lie and, with intermingled joy and pain, he begins to understand that there is no greater strength than daring to
be weak like this. Or possibly he himself falls in love. Flooded
with a strange feebleness, immense and surging like the sea, he
feels he is dying and yet loves his death.

Now perhaps we can better understand the contradictions of

adolescence: the melancholy, the anguish, the toughness and the spinelessness, the open rebellion and the timid tenderness, the generosity and all the selfishness. This is the decisive age when a young person is prompted to offer the gift of himself and equally tempted to remain a parasite for the rest of his life. For him, everything is confused—nostalgia for the pampering of childhood and a call to the generosity of adulthood, a yearning for uterine security and a yen for risk and adventure (he will swim an icy stream on a dare, but refuse to wash in the morning), sadness alternating with joy, the need to join others and the desire to keep to himself.

Let us follow this development further. The forces at work within will now orient him, beyond friends of his own sex, toward friends of the opposite sex. Vague and diffuse at first, this impulsion toward others will gradually fix itself upon girls without, however, being completely absorbed by them. Sexuality is always infinitely vaster than genitality. The adolescent boy will keep his male friends, but not as substitutes for female friends anymore; at the same time, he will love his old pals better because he no longer seeks from them what girls alone can contribute to his development.

And finally, among these girls, he will someday meet one whom he loves—that is, one who needs him, just as he confesses he needs her; one whose call will conjure up in his heart a power he never knew he possessed, just as she herself finds that, for the sake of this man who looks to her for everything, she is immeasurably better than she ever thought possible. They will create each other; their union will lift them above themselves; and their child will be but the manifestation, the proof and the sign of everything creative in their love. In him they will surpass themselves, for they would not love one another sufficiently unless they learned this new love.

Such a perfect evolution, sad to say, is rare. In fact, our psychological growth is constantly being threatened and marked by delay and regression. At every age, and even during so-called adulthood, we are tempted to withdraw into ourselves, lock everyone else out and seek our own pleasure in the very things that are meant to orient us toward others. For it is so much less troublesome to stay wrapped up in ourselves than to attach ourselves to others, so much easier to use them as instruments in our service than to devote ourselves to theirs.

Thus, for instance, a child of about three often starts sucking his thumb again. He abandoned this infantile habit months ago, but now, in a moment of grief or loneliness, after some frustration, an illness or a scolding, he may resume it. Observe what it means: longing for the maternal bosom, nostalgia for the parasitism of infancy. The hand which was fashioned to labor in the world, to act, to be extended to others and constitute the link between man and the universe—that hand he now draws fearfully toward himself and enjoys. What an abdication and what a symbol!

Well, sins of impurity—whether in adolescents or in grown-ups —are nothing but an inability to love, to act and go out of self, nothing but a timorous withdrawal into self. Every sin of impurity diminishes our power to love. We sin, not because we love someone too much, but because we do not love him enough. Notice the vicious circle that takes shape: inability to love causes impurity, and impurity causes egoism. Droves of people remain trapped in this infernal circle forever. To describe it adequately and show the way out would require a whole book on sex education. For now, let me say only that the sexual drive which occasions this havoc, works also—and principally—to repair it. Being too strongly sexed is not what makes a man sensual. Quite the opposite: nature does not run counter to grace; we are only too weak to respect the dynamism of each.

Suppression and Repression

Among the discoveries of modern psychology, the general public has latched onto several confused and dangerous notions—especially the need of avoiding repression. To many, this affords an excellent pretext to cast off all restraints and yield to their instincts.

Modern psychology, on the contrary, advises the suppression of instincts—that is, a sincere and conscious battle against them. Man and child alike must choose among the various kinds of activity that are open to them. If they choose lucidly and consonantly with the values they prize, they will spurn all others or at least find strength to renounce them.

I very often feel that, in the struggle against temptation, we should advise confrontation rather than flight. Fleeing temptations to which we know we would succumb is being prudent; but, otherwise, it is capitulating too soon, attributing excessive importance to them, underestimating and leaving untapped the forces of good. Instead, we should courageously face what we fear; then, pretending that we have yielded and pondering all the consequences, ask ourselves: "Am I happy now? Do I love myself and others better for this sin? Am I glad to have obtained what I hankered for?" Most of the time, we do not want that. We like to think about sin, but do not will to commit it. The proof is that we would be horrified at having carried out our fantasies and are sincerely glad we did not succeed. This means that we are less evil than we supposed, and that moral law is not a prohibition forced on us against our will, but the expression of our thinking nature and the aspiration of our better self.

Repression, on the other hand, is unconscious. It dictates conduct that cloaks itself in false motives; it suddenly assaults consciousness, which then has to justify surrendering; it fosters strange behavior, spawns infinite complications and condemns its victims to anxious puerility.

Occasionally we can observe the birth of these taboos: "If I get to the corner without stepping on the cracks in the sidewalk . . ." or "If I don't meet anyone from here to the next block, I'll do such and such a thing." The unconscious also offers an escape from decision-making for people who are afraid of their responsibilities and prefer to believe that they are driven, and excused, by events rather than assume the direction of them.

For example, a woman is tempted to cheat on her husband. When her psychologist asks, "Well, why don't you go ahead?" she exclaims, "How awful! Who ever heard of advising such a thing? It's forbidden." This is a typical misapprehension. The psychologist was merely trying to help her progress toward genuine moral conduct: no longer considering the commandment against adultery an arbitrary rule, her husband an obstacle to her happiness, and God a frowning policeman, but coming to perceive that she did not want to be unfaithful, because she loved her husband, because she desired to be free of the other man and because, down deep, she loved even him enough not to cause him any harm. She was capable of refusal but hoped to settle for repression.

Some parents breed repressions in a child by their premature demands. Too vulnerable to his parents, he reacts intensely to their indignation and their allegedly ethical censure of normal pleasures and exciting pastimes, such as playing with water or mud, with filth or dirty words. A child who does these things in all innocence may thus suffer a warping of his moral sense: from then on, his conduct will be determined by inexplicable but violent interdicts.

The requirements of neatness which grown-ups impose for their own convenience and satisfaction often exceed the child's physical capacities; and, what is worse, the accompanying reprobation exceeds his moral understanding. Since he confuses guilt and mere blundering, he deems himself condemned and condemnable, though blameless. He is so convinced of his culpability that he punishes himself. By sinking deeper into "evil," he becomes the executor of these verdicts, which he accepts without comprehending and carries out all the more blindly as he does not judge them.

Parents and Adolescents

The awkward age is especially a painful age—"the twilight of the gods." To a child, his parents are gods. No one is as strong as his father, no one as beautiful as his mother. His naive and absolute faith moves them to perform prodigies of love, generosity and devotion which they never guessed they could. "Evil as you are," says the Lord, "you can still be good to your children."

But at twelve or fourteen, a child discovers himself and his parents as well; he stands back and views them, for the first time, like strangers. Sincerely or not, he may imagine he is a foundling. Psychologically, it is true: he has just found himself and he feels strangely independent of his parents. The novelty of the experience automatically suggests this whole romantic fable.

Then he begins to judge his parents. Since he no longer identifies himself with them, he starts to hold different views and pursue different interests. Unanimity is out of the question now: the time has come for him to make a choice—an excruciating one. He has to achieve independence and assert himself as an individual; but the very thought troubles him, for he loves his parents and craves their love, and hurting them hurts him as much. Guilt-ridden on account of the disappointments which he causes them, he instinctively devises a way to punish himself—emphasizing his bad points, acting more objectionably than ever, and trying hard to place himself beyond the pale. His every action shouts, "I want to make you stop loving me and worrying about what happens to me. I can't stand seeing you bleed for me. Look, I'm no good; so leave me alone and let me suffer by myself."

If the parents understood what his behavior means, they would come running to console him for having been so obnoxious, to prove that his stratagem backfired, and to guarantee that, no matter what, they will never stop loving him.

An adolescent is a tragic person, mourning both his lost childhood and his parents. The more we love someone, the more we suffer when disappointed in him. That explains many of the dramas of adolescence: the bitterness, the hardness are only frustrated tenderness and admiration. However excellent parents may be, this crisis is normal. It is youth's first experience of the essential instability of creatures. "No man," observed the psalmist, "can be relied on." And, consequently, no father can hope to escape this verdict: sooner or later, he must necessarily let his children down, seem phony in their eyes and be judged accordingly. (This holds true—and much more so—of spiritual fatherhood: every priest, to whatever extent he remains a mere man, is a fraud.)

Instead of passively suffering because of their disillusioned child, instead of aggravating his guilt feelings with incessant reproaches or staying selfishly aloof in order to dull the pain, his parents should do everything in their power to help him. They cannot rest content with having given him life a dozen years ago, for the agony of childbirth is renewed at adolescence. But if they suffer aright, they will soon forget all their pangs for joy that a man is born into the world.

The parents ought to discover their inadequacy before the child does. His docility and tenderness delude them into thinking they can suffice him forever. But they must not remain children longer than he. Courageously, they themselves should orient him toward other friends and other adults, who can offer him what his own parents lack but nevertheless do give, in a sense, by making such contacts possible.

In this manner, when he turns toward others, he need not feel that he is abandoning his parents. They, in fact, are leading the way. Nor is he any longer the victim of their unconscious black-mail and infantile jealousy: "You're always gone. I know: you're not interested in us any more, you'd rather be with somebody else." Only too sensitive to such complaints, a youngster is torn by the choice they impose on him, instead of being permitted to reconcile loyalty with self-fulfillment.

For he must detach himself from his parents, just as a ripe apple pulls on its stem and gravitates toward liberation. They love him enough to remain attached to him for life, but their love should be deep enough and pure enough to understand the laws of his being and accept a break of which they personally feel no need. Tact will tell them to conceal their suffering lest it burden him with remorse and keep him hopelessly shackled even after the apparent separation.

For love of him, they should revive old friendships and resume occupations that they neglected when his dependence monopolized their time. Once more, they can begin to live and struggle and take their place among other adults. They ought to rival their own children in joy, zest and love of life, and teach them this supreme lesson (the exquisite fruit of their parenthood): "Life is worth living. All the sacrifices it entails can be a source of strength and renewed love. And by facing it with hope and sincerity, with generosity and confidence, you will grow closer to us than ever before."

Paradise Lost

Every stage in life is a birth and a death. We die to a familiar stability, to a peaceful and happy milieu in which we were comfortably settled; and we are born into a strange world where we have to test our new powers, alone and exposed to danger. At that point, we all react in one of two ways. When Adam and Eve were driven from the Garden of Eden, they had a choice: either to skulk around the outside, trying to recapture the past and, by chance or trickery, enjoy a few moments of pure happiness; or to turn their back on the place, go elsewhere and labor so as to reconstruct, through their mutual effort, something of that marvelous childhood which they remembered with nostalgia.

Life unceasingly demands of us the same genuine fidelity despite seeming detachments. Paradise is always ahead of us, not behind. We must neither forget it nor merely remember it, but believe that, with God's help, we can rebuild it.

II
Obedience

"Should children still obey their parents?" The question makes one smile, and yet it is paradoxical only on the surface. Many parents ask it. Modern child-training theory disconcerts them; and the more elaborate it grows, the more incompetent they feel. As laymen, they are reluctant to intrude upon a domain which has become technical. The example of "progressive" parents shocks but nevertheless sways them, so that, for fear of inducing complexes and repressions, they gradually revoke all constraints. What characterizes our era is its repudiation of authority pure and simple, and its titanic pursuit of freedom for races and peoples, for classes and man himself. Jean Lacroix, the psychoanalyst, describes this epoch as patricidal. Men today want to be brothers, but they are striving desperately to establish their brotherhood on the ruins of the very thing that unites them: fatherhood, authority, God.

Perhaps what our world lacks is a just notion of obedience, one that would conciliate the ideal of personal independence and that of social solidarity. Cardinal Mercier used to say, "Obedience is a noble act. It affirms the existence of a higher value than the individual's whims." Most of us obey only when we approve of the order given, little realizing that in so doing we never really obey at all. To obey is precisely to rise above ourselves and appeal to a superior reason—superior not only to our individual will but to our individual intellect—and deliberately become part of an order which lifts us beyond self.

This immediately answers the opening question. Bringing up a child is making him obey, helping him to rise above himself, and teaching him to love and want and do things which he does not spontaneously love or want or do—values which he will someday serve, just as they serve him.

Authority and Freedom

There is no insoluble conflict between authority and freedom. Any sensible upbringing should begin with a maximum of control and a minimum of liberty. To train somebody is to make oneself unnecessary, to teach a weaker person how to get along on his own. The educator—in the broadest sense of the word—has been defined as "a will that lends itself to others." Left to his own devices, a child is enslaved to instinct and caprice, but he can shake off that bondage if helped by a strong will from outside. Montalembert's comment on political liberalism applies to the rearing of children as well: "Between the powerful and the weak, the rich and the poor, it is freedom which oppresses and law which emancipates." Obedience makes a child do what he ought and really wants to do but never could if left unaided. Obviously, parents and teachers should not issue orders incessantly or arbitrarily but always gauge them according to the child's needs. Authoritarianism breaks and paralyzes the will or foments rebellion. That is why education—again, in the broadest sense—is an art: nothing else requires so much tact and foresight. Forgetting his personal ambitions and prejudices, an educator devotes himself passionately to the service of those entrusted to him. With all the skill at his command, he tries to envision their future, he helps them orient themselves toward their vocation, he teaches them to respect what is best in their nature; and if occasionally he dares to be harsh and unyielding, he does it convinced that he is acting with profound respect for those whom he knows and loves better than they know and love themselves.

Childhood is evidently the period in which training is indispensable. At that stage, a person is almost nothing by himself: he will become only what we bring him up to be. And, alas, bringing him up consists essentially in thwarting him; for this touchingly weak little being to whom our heart goes out is a tangle of impulses and vagaries, an unconsciously but terribly selfish and greedy person who must be bent, shaped, disciplined and humanized.

We can evaluate a method of training by measuring the time

that elapses between the manifestation and the satisfaction of a need. If you come running the moment your baby cries out, if you pick him up as soon as he starts screaming, if you feed him immediately when he is hungry, you are fostering a violent and weak egocentric. If you do not resist his furious and gluttonous howls as an infant, he will be insatiable and choleric as an adolescent and a man. Conversely, a child is lucky if, from the very beginning, he learns that the universe does not revolve around his little self and that he must wait, deserve and be grateful for the generous care that brings him a long-postponed gratification.

It is a pity that many parents nowadays cannot bear to make their child suffer for his own good, even for a second. They lack the courage to say, "No," and to punish when necessary. What with wars and calamities of all sorts, they have suffered so grievously that their hearts are too soft; the future looks so gloomy that they are eager to spoil its victims a trifle; and they have heard so many principles discussed that they no longer believe in much of anything. Contemplating the cathedral at Anvers, Heinrich Heine exclaimed, "Those people had dogmas. All we have is opinions, but opinions never built a cathedral." Unless parents have unshakable faith in the training they received and are themselves giving, they will be too weak to impose beneficial sacrifices.

Fathers and mothers must persuade themselves that it is their duty to secure obedience and not abandon a child to his whims. These may seem innocent because of the slight consequences at his tender age; but what will he do later if he follows the path he is being shown now, if he cannot wait or refuse himself anything? Moral rectitude is impossible without obedience to principles, in spite of temptation and fickleness.

Furthermore, the parents should literally embody principles which the child will learn to obey by example. "Don't dive into your plate like that; wait till everybody's been served. Always take the piece in front of you. Eat a little of everything. Sit straight and keep still. Answer when you're spoken to." All these regulations are much more important than we suppose; they concretize the order of justice, love and respect, which a child either heeds or learns to ignore completely.

The Will and Freedom

The chief goal in child training is inculcating strong habits, an indispensable condition for molding men of character. A strong will consists, not in perpetually asserting one's freedom, but in being able to rely on solid acquired habits when facing new situations.

Contrariwise, a weak will lacks the support of such habits, balances in endless indecision, deliberates about everything and calls even the obvious into question.

If we must appeal to our free will for trivial everyday decisions like rising, dressing, washing up, scheduling meals and work, and so forth, we fritter away our energy. But if, in all such matters, we follow a rule that has become habitual, we husband our energy for more important matters.

A child who has been brought up improperly has to be told the most elementary things over and over because his parents have not implanted habits in him. "Get up; come on, get up. Wash your feet. Look at what you're doing: you're putting your right shoe on your left foot. Clean your fingernails. Hold your head up. Don't drag your heels. Blow your nose." He will always be a jellyfish because he has not acquired habits through obedience.

I do not wholly subscribe to the adage: "Before commanding, one must be able to obey." I would modify it and say, "One must be able to obey before he can disobey." The only disobedience which deserves consideration is that of a person who is capable of obeying and has proved it. Anything else is an insipid piece of cowardice.

Although it is desirable to discuss with little ones even when they are quite young, to justify an order and show them that we are reasonable so that they, also, may learn to reason, still we must not give them more freedom than they can handle or make them responsible for their behavior. Wise parents encourage a child to know what he wants and allow him to choose for himself as often as possible, but they realize that they are often duty-bound to will and decide for him. He, in turn, appreciates this exercise of authority, for, as we said earlier, it reassures, stabilizes and stimulates him.

Of course, they do not issue edicts at the drop of a hat; and much less do they repeat an order and ceaselessly complain because it has not been executed. Instead—and this takes a little imagination—they adopt a few solid and practical sanctions which they will apply firmly at the first "No." This is the critical moment in child training. As soon as a youngster knows that he can get out of obedience by grumbling, debating, coaxing or temporizing, all is lost.

Sanctions are not popular at present. All the same, they are necessary; or, rather, they become unnecessary only when they have been used designedly. Everyone today knows the theory behind conditioned reflexes. A reflex (such as salivation) that is regularly set off by a certain stimulus (such as the sight of food) can likewise be set off by other stimuli if they, too, have been sufficiently associated with that reflex (for example, if the sound of a bell immediately precedes meals, eventually the mere ringing will activate the salivary glands—even if there is no meal). Similarly, if a child associates a certain look or tone of voice with the punishment that he dreads (perhaps a spanking or some privation), the day will soon come when this look or tone will be enough to produce the desired intimidation without recourse to further steps.

But many parents are short on imagination. They have never taken ten minutes' thought to organize a practical arsenal of sanctions, with the result that they are caught unprepared or driven by anger to lash out with excessive and indefensible penalties.

Punishment is never very pleasant to mete out. In punishing a child, the parents themselves suffer; but they will suffer far worse someday if they fail to punish him now.

How To Obtain Obedience

Obviously, there is a right way and a wrong way to obtain obedience. Do not give too many orders or too many reprimands. Otherwise, how can you expect a child to take them seriously?

Before decreeing a measure, check yourself and remain silent; then calmly weigh what it will cost your child to respect it, and you to impose and uphold it. If, after that, you deem it worth the trouble involved, go ahead. From the tone of your voice he will sense that you have carefully considered the matter and are determined to see it through. Your thoughtful resoluteness will impress him, since children are more sensitive to the tone than to the meaning of words. Many remarks (especially "Keep quiet!") communicate nothing to them but the parents' nervousness. Along with an order, you should impart to your child the strength, the calmness and the resolve with which you have decided on it and by which he will be enabled to obey.

Give him enough fun, enough relaxation and leeway to warrant your being severe on other points. Demand insistently, but do not demand too much. Here, fathers in particular tend to exaggerate. In their desire to be proud of their offspring, especially a son, they fabricate an ideal that is out of keeping with his age and resources or, sometimes, even with their own past. Since they have no more time to become children with their child, they want him prematurely to become a man like them. Disappointed and irritated, they lay the whole blame on him; and the more they love him in their own fashion, the more they resent his frustrating them so badly.

The right way to love a child is to love him, not as he is or *should* become, but as he *can* become, and to furnish him all the help (strictness and tenderness both) which will lessen the divergence between both directions.

True Independence

All these observations about obedience were meant only to prepare the way for a discussion about independence. A child has to learn obedience; but an adolescent has to serve a far more important apprenticeship and a far more difficult one—that of autonomy.

Unskilled educators generally do the opposite: because a child is easier to handle, they let him be; and because an adolescent is more rebellious, they want to break and coerce him. This is the spirit of contradiction, not a method of tutelage. No doubt, an adolescent should still obey; in fact, he should obey even more than a child, but differently and better. The purpose of training always remains the same: obedience to principles rather than inclinations. For a child, principles are incarnate in his parents. An adolescent, however, can grasp the reason behind a rule; and, above all, he can love and want that rule because of the good which it procures or safeguards. His parents' duty is to initiate him into this authentic obedience which produces authentic independence.

Of all God's gifts, none is more beautiful than freedom. It is superior to life itself, and parents should note and admire the first manifestations of their child's need for independence with as much joy as they once watched for his first smile or sign of recognition.

What will he become later if he is not independent? A man of character is an independent man—independent of his instincts and his emotions, of his surroundings and of current prejudices. He obeys neither from fear nor from self-interest nor even—yes, mothers!—from affection, but solely from conviction. By contrast, a weakling is one who follows the crowd, however mistaken it may be. As a committee member, he votes resolutions because, at the decisive moment, his scruples seem inopportune; as a politician, he lends an ear only to the majority; as a citizen, he consistently backs the causes that catch the popular fancy; and so on, and so on.

How can we immunize a child against this nauseating docility? How help him to become a man of character—that is, one who can resist as well as comply? Fénelon warned that children should not be turned into "spineless souls."

A true educator loves and looks for self-determination. He is happy when he sees that his charges have grown thoroughly independent of him and yet remain docile, friendly and grateful. They obey him, not because they love and fear him, but because they are deeply devoted to the principles which he respects and has taught them to respect. Parents should command in the name of the principles they themselves observe, and should gradually initiate their child into the religion of those principles. Thus there will no longer be an odious subordination of one man to another, but a communion of two persons who join freely to worship the same God. "Anyone who listens to you listens to me . . . and whoever sees me sees the Father."

Though it is the parents' duty to make sure that they are obeyed, they ought nonetheless to guard against an oppressive conception of their authority—which, above all, is meant to liberate.

An adolescent is highly impressionable and influenceable, much more sensitive and much less balanced than a child. On reading this, mothers will protest, "Oh, my boy was far more affectionate when he was younger!" No, he was just more spontaneous and showed his feelings uninhibitedly. In the adolescent, affectivity runs deeper, though the manifestations of it are more restrained. He can now control his emotions better and uses this new power for two purposes: very often, to mask his feelings and, sometimes, to work out a more personal and meaningful way of expressing them. Yet, under that mask of indifference, what a frightful ebulliency—elation and gloom, ardor and regret, desire and disgust, impulsiveness and belligerence. This is the period of intense friendships, adventurous dreams, timidity and melancholy.

Precisely when and because adolescents are inwardly confused, God gives them this instinct for freedom, this need of reasoning, of conquering and governing themselves which is the most precious instrument that an educator can use to help them at this stage.

Many parents misinterpret the situation, since the expression of this need for independence is obviously directed against them first and foremost. Just as puppies gnaw at whatever can exercise their new teeth, so adolescents clash blindly with anything that offers resistance—and, before all else, their parents, who then defend themselves by damming the nascent need instead of channeling it toward genuine satisfaction.

The teen-ager who is so arrogant at home is afraid of water, people, his own pals, cold, heat, everything; he would rather die than wear a hat, walk to school with his sister, admit that his parents cannot afford a car, or be seen making the sign of the cross in public. In a word, he is a poor, miserable funk. But all the same, he feels a desperate urge to take a chance, to assert himself, to use his will. His parents ought to rejoice, for here is the opportunity of a lifetime, here is hope that he may escape the general atmosphere of mediocrity and cowardice. If they stimulate that urge adroitly, exercise and nourish it, give it proper goals and reward it, if they cultivate that instinct like their most precious possession, they will succeed in creating a man.

Guiding these adolescents is a difficult but thrilling art because they are so sensitive, so vulnerable and so contradictory. Many parents are dismayed, since they no longer recognize the caressing, tractable child whom they once learned to love. Now they must learn to love another, who is certainly more complex but much more captivating, and who needs them fully as much as when he was younger.

An adolescent has no faith in himself. That is why he asserts himself so fiercely and so stupidly. He needs a prop and keeps looking for one, but he will accept help only from people who treat him like the man he aspires to become.

First, he needs intellectual help. When a child does not know, he asks; when a teen-ager does not know, he pontificates. Strange to say, this denotes progress—or, rather, the possibility of progress. No longer satisfied with the peremptory dicta of grown-ups, he wants to find his own answers; and, in the process, he goes from passivity to activity, from the happy parasitism of childhood to a virile ambition for autonomy. But his categorical judgments come from radio or this morning's paper; he has read every syllable of what he says or heard it from a friend, which is enough for him to assert it against all comers—that is, to assert himself.

Contradicting him is useless: he will only become angry or close up. Ridiculing him is even worse: he will grow headstrong and, without saying another word, go out to seek in his cronies or a girl friend the ready audience his father and mother deny him.

What to do? Help him. Start by not colliding with him head on. You are exasperated, burning to call him an idiot and damn his views out of hand. Keep still, swallow your indignation, calm down and then tell him that his opinions, though they may sound stupid at first, are quite interesting. Learn to chat with him on equal terms. If you treat him like a child, you lose all influence over him precisely when he needs it more than ever before.

A teener listens only to people who make him feel like a serious and intelligent man, even—and especially—if he does not deserve it. Still, this is the only way to help him become one. Try to remember some of the ideas you had at his age; tell him about them and explain how you were brought to change your mind. Rather than reject his theories en bloc, introduce clarifying distinctions, and both of you will soon arrive at an acceptable truth.

Here, as in most domains, exigency precedes capacity. A boy needs to be treated like a man before he can act like one, precisely because that is the only way he will become one. Your son wants to think for himself though he does not know how to think at all. If you dismiss him with scorn or anger, where do you expect him to acquire the skill that you reproach him for lacking? At the movies? In the newspaper? From his buddies? You are the ones who should teach him how to think—and you can, provided you discuss with him calmly and patiently. Someday, you will be rewarded for it: though he has always attacked your most cherished ideas in your presence, you will hear him defending them in his own circle and expounding them better than you ever could.

Secondly, your son needs guidance. He nobly aspires to regulate his conduct for himself, and you hope he will eventually succeed. Meanwhile, there are better things to do than oppose or deride him. Tactfully suggest what reasonable conduct is. Instead of saying, "Do this," ask him what he would like to do. He will be dumbfounded because, though he is sure he wants something different from what you want, he rarely knows what. Outline the various attitudes that are possible in a given situation and explain why you so admire a particular one. Try to entrust responsibilities to him before he usurps them and while he is still young enough to be proud and grateful, to appreciate your advice and accept criticism. Stimulate his initiative by giving him something with which to work or create and by being interested in his projects. Double every dollar he saves, and enter into freely ratified contracts with him. Give him a room or at least a nook of his own. Surround yourselves with friends who have sons and daughters of his age so that he need not seek companions elsewhere and alone. Then you can afford to be liberal about his peregrinations and the company he keeps.

Perhaps you do all that and are still disappointed. You see no results. Your son is nondescript or outlandish, unstable or heartless. Do not lose hope.

Bringing up children requires patience and optimism. To help yourselves along, you should each recall your own case. Did we not all spend our entire youth fighting our parents on a thousand trivial fronts which, to us, symbolized our personal independence: slamming doors or leaving them open, refusing to wash before meals, letting our dirty clothes lie where they fell, and so on? And now you find yourselves imposing these same regulations on your children with utter faith in an imperative that comes, beyond you, from the very parents against whom you battled for so long. Do not worry: your children will do the same. Because you do not allow their resistance to discourage you, someday, when they themselves grapple with life and their fellowman and their own children, someday they will resemble you.

III
Instilling a Sense
of Religion

Nature and Importance

Religious sense is the faculty of perceiving and appreciating the things of God. To make Christians out of our children, it will not suffice to have them memorize prayers and answers from the catechism or observe rules and practice rites. All this is necessary but will probably remain ineffectual unless we succeed in giving them a taste for God.

"The only ideas that actuate us," wrote Maurice Barrès, "are those that make us weep." Indeed, we do nothing well unless we love it. Saint Peter concludes a long list of spiritual counsels by stating the indispensable condition for implementing them: having "tasted the goodness of the Lord."

The pure of heart shall see God. Unhappily for us, there is no purity without purification—that is, without education in purity. Our hearts are filled with everything but God; we live on impressions and emotions that are almost always profane; and trifles—a blunder, a failure, a snub or a smile—upset us for days at a time. But God and the things of God do not move or interest us. His joy consists in revealing himself, in making himself known to us; but, in spite of his omnipotence, he cannot do so if we are engrossed and blinded by everything except him. The saints differ from us in that they are careful to recognize and perpetuate the impressions that come to them from God, whereas we let these same ideas and emotions slip away, thrilling to them for a moment but then becoming absorbed in others. A whole natural and supernatural upbringing is needed to give us "a sense of the true and a

37

taste for the good," to make us relish and savor and experience the sapidity of things divine instead of calling them insipid.

So many Christians want to believe, so many refuse to disbelieve. Yet talk to them about God, prayer or the Gospels, and it all seems meaningless: they do not react, and the only sign of life and volition they show is to walk away.

Others truly believe and laboriously strain to reach God through dry prayers, cold communions and dull reading. Their merit is enormous, their aridity valiant; they deserve esteem and are certainly worth more than impulsive sentimentalists. But they have a right to complain that their upbringing has but imperfectly developed their latent powers. Not sufficiently motivated by faith, hope and love, they lack the dispositions that would make the action of grace in them quick and easy. Consequently, the Holy Spirit (whose proper work is enkindling, consoling, rejoicing and teaching) can operate in them only feebly, as though his gifts found little there to contact or energize—his gifts of wisdom, knowledge, understanding and counsel, which are all designed to pierce through, ponder and illuminate God's mysteries; his gift of fortitude, which communicates spiritual intrepidity; his gift of piety, which is an inclination and a readiness to honor God and love him like a Father; and his gift of fear, which makes supernatural realities so vivid and significant that we conceive a holy respect for them. These gifts of the Spirit are necessary for salvation. If they are absent or left unused, our animal nature cannot love the things of God but only those of earth; but if we live according to the Spirit, we come to treasure the things that are above.

A Difficult Task

Good teachers are rare. Few can awaken in their pupils the particular "sense" to which their field of study is directed. For example, a lecturer can discourse on masterpieces indefinitely without inculcating a sense of beauty. You meet erudite musicologists, professors in conservatories and brilliant virtuosi who are devoid of musical sense. A crusader who is sincerely moved by the misery of the lower classes may have a smattering of social theories but lack all social sense. An instructor in business administration, happily or unhappily, can be short on business sense. But, worst of all, we know prizewinners in catechism, and even theology experts, who have no religious sense. Surely there is nothing more difficult to rouse and nurture. How can we collaborate with the Master who works secretly within souls, and harmonize our teaching with his plans? It takes an artist or a mother to make a child aware of his deepest needs and predilections, to show him the secret of recollecting himself and listening so that he may penetrate further into what he knows and translate his "inarticulate groans" into accurate language.

Say a child goes into church alone. Surprised at first by his own audacity, he holds his breath and sits there as mute and motionless as a statue. After a while, he relaxes and moves a bit, astonished by the enormous volume of silence, which outside noises amplify rather than destroy; and he slowly becomes attuned to all that peace and solemnity. He looks about, thinks and contemplates. The calmness both overpowers and uplifts him, and he is just about to perceive what grace is producing in his heart when a grown-up enters, sees him doing nothing and concludes that he is not praying. "What are you doing there? Say a prayer." So the child recites a Hail Mary and hurries out.

All too many people have hurried out like that. In fact, when someone shows interest in religious matters or quizzes me about them, I immediately peg him as an unbeliever, for he is still curious. So were our children once. What has blunted them?

Secularism

The period from which today's marvelous religious renaissance is helping us to emerge has been characterized by secularism—a loss of the sense of sacredness. To Alexis Carrel, the atrophy of that sense is just as harmful as the atrophy of the intellect. "The sense of sacredness," he wrote, "is almost completely neglected, and the atrophying of these fundamental activities has made modern man spiritually blind." A few decades before, Péguy declared, "This appalling dearth of sacredness is, beyond a doubt, the hall-mark of our contemporary world."

The greatest obstacle to the spiritual life of young people now-adays is that they are living in a profane world, a deconsecrated world. To acquire and preserve a religious frame of mind, they have to stop breathing, check all their nourishment and purify every influence. According to Abbé Moeller, there is no longer any such thing as Christendom, but only Christians. We cannot live our religion unless we withdraw. Very significantly, the chief religious exercise of modern times consists in going away, in retreating from the world, so as to seek, somewhere outside of it, a normal, sacred atmosphere.

To the adolescent of today, this world looks bright and simple, like a modern efficiency apartment. Nothing in the human city transcends, terrifies or elevates him. There is no more mystery, no more nature, and practically no more art—just wall-to-wall ar-tificiality. Contrasting our streamlined cities with those of the Orient, where one can hardly take a step without seeing an altar, a temple, an image or an inscription—in other words, some wit-ness to the presence of an invisible world—Paul Claudel saw at home nothing but "bourgeois stores, silo-like apartment buildings, and barrels and barrels of human sauerkraut." How can anyone there awaken to that blend of terror and admiration and ineffable love which constitutes the sense of sacredness? Even religious ceremonies no longer enkindle it.

Let me give you an example. Every Sunday evening at our school, I observe a characteristic scene. When it comes time for Benediction and the students go to chapel, the main quadrangle which they cross is crowded with cars—beautiful American ones, sleek and lustrous under the lights. As if mesmerized, the boys stop and group in circles around their favorite makes, comparing, commenting, displaying wide erudition and occasionally reaching out a reverent hand to touch. Their hearts pound with emotion: they have rediscovered the sense of sacredness. Then they trudge into chapel. But their act of worship is over, so they make a sketchy genuflection and settle down stolidly in their pews. From its simple gilded monstrance among the flowers and candles, the pale host cannot fix the glances that rove distractedly in search of something to look at. Where are those fastbacks, those long, low hoods with their intoxicating promise of power, those coldly imperious head-lights?

Clearly, in our modern world, religion is becoming more and more of an individual phenomenon, something that has to be lived against the stream. But youth is the time when one is most sensi-tive to trends and influences. As a result, our young people suffer from a divided allegiance. When we describe authentic Christian living to them, they admire it but find it impossible to imitate in their milieu. Though often they esteem religion and would want to believe, they feel that, in spite of themselves, they are and must remain pagans: there would be too much to change, too much to react against. If, in religion class, they pose objections and spon-taneously side with the doubters, it is not hostility that animates them but a desire to hold us responsible for the divorce between "real life" and religious principles. Actually, their conscience is troubling them because they realize that they are governed by their era much more than by their faith. They imagine they would have to turn everything upside down, but very few have any inclination or courage to do so. And the prospect of going through life torn between two irreconcilable tendencies distresses them: they are unwilling to sacrifice one and sure that they will never be strong enough to resist the other.

The Family

Hence there is only one milieu that makes religious training pos-sible, only one that effectively guards the soul against secular in-fluences, only one that shields and feeds the flame of religious life—the family. In his own home, the poorest of men is master. What propaganda, public manifestations, official decrees, and even courses and sermons cannot accomplish, the family accomplishes by living its life in all simplicity. No one else possesses a father's or a mother's power to reveal God to their little ones and create an environment where they breathe sacredness.

A very understandable but dangerous campaign has convinced many parents that their essential religious duty is to send their children to a Catholic school. They still provide elementary religious formation, but even some devout ones behave as if their task were over and their competence nullified from the day their child first goes to school. Yet daily experience proves that neither a Catholic school nor parish-sponsored activities can replace the Christian family. Indeed, the school actually suffers from the exaggerated confidence placed in it, since the swelling ranks of those who no longer receive religious instruction at home prevent it from fulfilling the family's expectations. The parents' reliance on parochial schools is justified only if limited, and the schools' work can be solid only if seconded by the parents.

As a matter of fact, a child learns best from what he sees. The older we grow, the more we are astonished at the lasting effect of our early training, the one which our parents imparted mainly by being and doing. I am afraid that with adolescence, and especially maturity, we stop learning: the more we are taken up with our work, the less we absorb. The best time to assimilate the art of living is in childhood, that period of trust, blissful leisure and malleability when basic habits are ingrained, indelible memories stamped, and family traditions transmuted into firm convictions.

Contrary to popular opinion, what influences your child at this age is not your harangues, not your counsels and, I daresay, not even your example, but what you are and what you live for. He, too, will live for that—and nothing else. "A child," notes Abbé Caffarel, "breathes in, eats and drinks his parents' life. To whatever degree they are physically, morally and spiritually alive, he himself begins to live. Child rearing is a transfusion, not of blood, but of life."

All of us who bring up children should tell ourselves, "They live exactly the way we do." That terrifying truth makes us wish we were more completely alive; it fills us with shame and anxiety, for, although we might accept our mediocrity if it stopped with us, we vehemently refuse to pass it on to them. "Improve yourself, and you improve the world," runs the old saying. A challenge for anyone, it becomes an absolute duty for parents and teachers, since we cannot bring up our children unless we uplift ourselves. "I sanctify myself for them," said Jesus, "so that they also may be sanctified in truth."

The fundamental reason for this duty is that God first reveals himself to your children through you. When he wanted to tell mankind who he was, what to call him and how to picture him, he showed himself as the Father. Your children's young minds and hearts, then, fashion God in your image and guess his attributes from your virtues. Their notion of him will always smack of you. And unless, in later life, they can draw upon childhood memories and family experiences for the images, ideas and sentiments that make God a living person, every educator who works with them will feel that his teaching has fallen on sterile, stony ground.

For a long time, your children thought you were almighty: there was nothing you could not do or understand, no problem you could not cope with, no difficulty you could not brush away with a flick of the wrist. When our youngest boarders are confined to the infirmary, they often sigh: "If Mom were here, she'd cure me fast." Only in his family can a child acquire this fundamentally religious disposition of trust in Another's omnipotence.

Justice, too, is a family experience. Elsewhere, the child sees nothing but injustice. At school, the top student often succeeds with only half a try, whereas the plugger frequently fails; at play, the brawniest always wins though he is not necessarily the best sport; and people in authority sometimes let themselves be hoodwinked by hypocrites or impressed by sham qualities. But at home, everyone shows his true colors, receives what he deserves, and is soon put back in his place if he tries to usurp another's. Deep in his heart, every child has a passion for justice and dreams of an impartial Judge, but he will come to believe unshakably in God's justice only after years of experiencing yours.

Above all, however, homelife can teach children that there is such a thing as love and that the true force which moves the world and bestows happiness is this very love—not (as children with a deficient upbringing imagine) money, violence, gadgets or guns.

We keep repeating "God is love," but what can they know about either unless they learn to recognize and appreciate and return love in their own home?

The same love that brought them into this world should continue to nourish and strengthen them. Their religious training demands that you love one another more, that you love them more, and that they become increasingly aware of your mutual affection, thoughtfulness, trust and respect, so that these may be for them the reflection and revelation of another love. If you want to make them more religious, be more complete fathers and mothers, show them love and esteem directly inspired by the heart of God. You have been entrusted with a formidable mission—revealing the Father; and it is incumbent on both of you because father and mother together manifest the Father, his might and his tenderness, his dominion and his gentleness. Only those children who have known paternal force and benevolence can form a just idea of the Father.

Begetting and educating children obliges all of us, parents and teachers, to take refuge in the Father and nestle close to him in order that we may ceaselessly recharge our love from his, beg him to enter into us so as to love them as they need to be loved, and earnestly commit to his care these frail lives which make even our best efforts seem so feeble.

In turning to the Father thus, out of desire for a truer and deeper fatherhood, we discover a dynamic incentive to intensify our own spiritual life. Accordingly, we who are evil manage to be good to our children, and we who do not know the Father (for "no one knows him") enter into the secrets, the intimacy and the nature of him from whom all fatherhood, whether natural or spiritual, derives its name. Our love for our children will reveal the Father to us also; and, because of our need and our determination to love them better, we shall all the more fervently beg the Son, "Lord, show us the Father."

By means of our new love, which affords them a glimpse of the Father's love and power and delicacy, we shall initiate our children into their filial status. When they realize that they are loved with a love which comes from the depths of God's heart and which, through them, is directed back to him, they will feel compelled to live as his sons, to become the Son; quite naturally, they will be brought up in the beautiful condition of children of God and bear the traits of their exalted family.

Saint John's Gospel contains a whole treatise on education which outlines the dispositions we should cultivate in children so that they may learn to resemble the Son: first of all, confidence ("I know that you always hear me. . . . The Father loves the Son and shows him everything he does himself"); second, submission ("I always do what pleases him"); third, inward attention ("As I hear, so do I judge"); and, fourth, pride ("The Father and I are one").

At times, when fathers come to my office and complain about their children, I feel like quoting two verses from that same Gospel: "I tell you most solemnly, the Son can do nothing by himself; he can do only what he sees the Father doing. . . . For the Father loves the Son and shows him everything he does himself . . . and whatever the Father does, the Son does too." Rarely does a father have the patience or take the time to show his sons what he does and what they also must learn in order to do whatever he does. This would be a first introduction to real work and strength of character. Many a father who toils assiduously has lazy children simply because he never bothered to show them what he was doing or what they themselves should do. Frequently, his only concern off the job is to provide luxurious surroundings where he may find rest from his labor, but where his children learn only idleness and extravagance. Let us face the truth: courageous, devoted, persevering parents often make a child's life so easy and agreeable that, far from guiding him along the same narrow path, they prevent him from acquiring a single quality which helped them to succeed.

This holds even truer of prayer and the spiritual life. Parents are quite mistaken in thinking that their traditional religion—embalmed and preserved as it is, with no struggle or problems—will suffice their child. If he is worth his salt, he will necessarily think for himself and question long-standing habits; if he has a spark of personality, he needs to find in his parents a living, active, militant religion. There is no use having him recite his prayers unless both father and mother join in and sincerely pray with him, instead of just pretending and taking part in a sort of childish game, for he would be the first to see through it and balk at the artificiality of it all.

We exhort children to observe the Lord's day fittingly, but for most of them Sunday at home is the dreariest day of the week. There are two extremes to be avoided here. Some parents have a single desire: to rest and divert themselves; and, since the children are not interested in lounging, they are dragged along to restaurants and theaters for adult distractions that mean nothing to the young. Other parents may be active Catholics who busy themselves with pious works, retreats and various forms of Catholic Action. With the father or the mother continually absent, the children are left to themselves, and nothing is done to plan their Sunday. The right way to hallow Sunday is to spend it together as a family, happy to be reunited after a week's work and eager to revivify mutual love through recreations that please everyone.

To raise others is to raise oneself first. You can make of your children only what you make of yourselves. If you expect them to change, you must be willing to change too; if you want to draw them closer to God, you must resemble him more; if you want them to become like the Son, you must become like the Father.

Prayer

Never set out to teach your children how to pray until they themselves ask you to.

The whole art of education lies in awakening need and desire, not forcing someone who has no appetite. In religious instruction, specifically, our worst mistakes are authoritarianism and overfeeding. We cram the whole of Christian doctrine down a youngster's throat and inject massive doses of the sacraments into him, like a reserve supply, in case he does not want any more when he reaches eighteen. The result is usually lasting aversion. Boys and girls who graduate from our CCD classes, and especially from our schools, generally need two or three years—often longer—to get over their feeling of satiety and loathing.

We should also avoid lecturing them prematurely on sound versus unsound religion, lest they reject both together. Better to wait; for, if there is anything worse than the unbeliever's questions without answers, it is the catechist's answers without questions. For most of our pupils, we might revise the Our Father from "Give us this day our daily bread" to "Give us this day a better appetite, a bit of curiosity about you, a little interest in you!"

At present, many Catholic educators are vainly trying to water down their demands in order to win their pupils over; but even if the daily Mass requirement is reduced to two Masses a week or one a week or only one a month, it is always too much for nauseated and refractory stomachs. A wise mother knows the cause of ano-rexia: when her baby no longer cares to eat, she realizes that she has been oversolicitous about feeding him. Far too many adoles-cents suffer from a similar loss of appetite in spiritual matters. I could almost wish for a Truce of God, a moratorium on all re-ligious instruction, so that, someday, as mature men and women, they might seek it on their own.

Some parents, in order to salve their conscience and, often, to wax sentimental, promptly teach their little one the mere gestures and formulas of piety. They "make him pray."

That is exactly the wrong way to proceed. Authoritarianism in adults inevitably breeds resistance and rebellion in children. Since every action entails reaction, your child will sooner or later oppose whatever you impose. This explains the customary scenes which accompany family prayer or, worse yet, the children's prayer: turmoil, uncontrollable giggling, eccentricities and the thousand means by which youngsters manifest their nonparticipation in what is commanded.

Parents love to talk nonsense with their children, but the chil-dren do not like it. What they want is to become like adults—peo-ple who pray when they wish and, consequently, often do not pray. The only way to teach children to pray is for the parents them-selves to pray: pray for their own sake, from conviction and need, not from a desire to "give good example." I do not know of a single child who, unless warped by tyranny or indulgence, does not dream of becoming like his father or mother. Similarly, I do not know of a single child who, unless disgusted at having had prayer forced on him, does not ask to join in his parents' prayer. He sees that praying is something grown-ups do; it appeals to him, and participation becomes a privilege. If both father and mother pray and regularly withdraw to recollect themselves and read scripture together in the next room, you can be sure that he will hover nearby, naively imitate them and ask to do the same.

I know more than one mother who is clever enough to tell her three- or four-year-older before entering into church, "Mommy's going in to pray. It'll be too quiet for you, so she'll walk you back home first." Invariably, he begs to stay with her. She lets herself be convinced but tells him to nudge her when he wants to leave. Inside, she prays without heeding him, for she knows that making him recite a prayer could break the spell. He watches and apes her for a while, looks around, takes a few noiseless steps and comes back. And it sometimes happens that when she rises to leave after fifteen minutes' silence, this frisky little imp asks, "Already? It's so good to be here!"

I also know a pastor who wisely runs a Sunday-morning baby-sitting service, next door to church, for children ranging from a few months to twelve years of age. Whenever a youngster is allowed to decide where he will spend Mass time, he unfailingly goes over to play once or twice but always ends up preferring to accompany his family. (It is only fair to add that these are lively Masses where he can see his parents pray by singing, taking part and marching in procession.)

The umbilical cord only seems to have been cut. A child prays in his mother's womb, in symbiosis with his father. Anything less is liable to be hypocritical and repugnant.

When a child, whether he be seven or twenty, balks at Sunday Mass, the only sensible reply runs something like this: "I'll never force you to go to Mass. After all, the Lord doesn't want to see drudges, recalcitrants or prisoners; he invites sons and daughters. Naturally, it takes a while to understand him and enjoy meeting him. If anything, it took me even longer than you. All the same, Mass isn't a matter of whim, and I don't want you making a scene about it every week. All I ask is that you think this over, and we'll discuss it calmly some evening. You'll tell me what you've decided to do for the next six months; and if you honestly feel you should stay away from Mass, I assure you God understands and will wait for you forever. But, in that case, I'd ask you not to cut yourself off from what your mother and I hold to above all else. At least, read a book on the subject, let me analyze your problem with you now and then, or come with us and listen to a particularly solid talk on religion."

What about mortal sin, then? For your children, you are the Church. And you have the responsibility of so training them that they will go to Mass voluntarily at the age of twenty, when they are ready to leave home. This is a long-distance race, not a sprint, so do not allow yourselves or them to become winded. Surely the Church does not intend that you should coerce them till they rebel, but that you should nurture convictions in them which will outlive mechanical habits.

These remarks may sound as if I have repudiated all discipline and joined the ranks of "modern" educators. On the contrary, I firmly believe in discipline and obligation and even punishment—but everywhere except the domain of religion. It is too sacred, too near conscience for anyone to trespass there, armed with authority: you cannot accomplish anything worthwhile in matters of faith unless you obtain interior assent. The Second Vatican Council proclaimed religious freedom and respect for the conscience of unbelievers. It is high time we also started respecting the freedom and conscience of young Catholics.

As was said above, our true teacher of religion is the Holy Spirit, whose principal function, through his gifts, is to make us relish the things of God—in other words, appreciate what is good and not find religious activities vapid.

With the youth of today, you have achieved nothing if you have merely compelled them to receive the sacraments and observe the commandments of the Church. In our time, we were still tractable enough to submit conscientiously; and, once led to Mass by a sense of obligation, we sometimes managed to pray sincerely, though we would not have gone or prayed of our own accord. But the present generation bristles at the very thought of constraint. And not only the young, but everybody. What Frenchman or what American, for example, respects authority—civil, military or religious—simply because it is authority? Everything is being questioned everywhere. Would it not be insincere of you to enjoin on your children what you yourselves do not accept?

Let us stop calling upon the secular arm (even if it is ours!) in religious matters. God desires to speak to the hearts of your children through your example, through the radiance of your faith and the testimony of your prayer. He has ways of his own—the ways of love: he proposes but never imposes himself on anyone. Your children will hear him just like you, if you have heard him.

This is the method exemplified in the Gospels. When Christ undertook the religious training of his followers, he did not stipulate prayers, rosaries or set services. Rather, he himself prayed, alone, for long stretches, and often the whole night through. And one morning as he returned, serene and luminous, his apostles drew near and asked, "Lord, teach us how to pray."

The secret of religious training is to make our children want to become like us, like people who pray.

Gestures, Persons and Things

A child learns only by doing: he must do in order to know. What he thinks, he automatically mimes. Especially of children is the old adage true: "Act the way you think, or you will eventually think the way you act." Scores of children come to school without having learned prayerful gestures and reverent attitudes. Their whole demeanor is pagan: they make themselves comfortable anywhere; they enter chapel—and leave it, especially—with the same quick, conquering stride as on the playground; they caricature a genuflection and sit in their pew as if they were at the movies.

Religion must enter into their bodies before it can enter into their minds. We should teach them to carry themselves worshipfully, to clasp their hands, to walk with reverence, to breathe slowly, to keep silence and then listen to it. They will have learned a precious lesson if they understand that even walking is praying. Saint Francis Xavier converted the Japanese by the way he walked. Seeing him move about, silent, recollected and full of joyous gravity, no one could ignore the Presence he lived in and conversed with interiorly. Youngsters are so easily impressed that respect and admiration come to them naturally. With that predisposition working for them, they can easily be educated to reverence, which is the most exquisite token of love. As beneficial to those who teach as to those who learn, what a prodigious mission it is to reveal to children everything sacred in this world, along with the awe they should feel for it—bread, beauty, nature, their own work and that of others, but also and especially the poor, the aged, the weak, the outcast and God.

Sacred Scripture

In addition to the religious teaching normally and naturally absorbed from family life, other forms of divine revelation await your children. After helping them imbibe God in your home, teach them to recognize him in his book and his sacraments, in his cult, his images and his representatives.

To that end, tell them about the gradual manifestation of God's love, starting in Eden, where he often came in the cool of the evening and began to reveal himself in familiar conversation with Adam. Next, show how Adam interrupted that dialogue and how God resumed it through the prophets until the day he finally spoke to us through his Son—the day the Word became flesh in order to stay with us, entrusted and handed over to us forever.

Dwell on the good people who nevertheless suffered and were persecuted—Abel, Joseph, Moses, Isaac, David and (why not?) Socrates—for those splendid narratives will prepare your children to understand and love the Just One.

Forget everything you think you know about the Gospels; then, with an imaginative reading that is the highest form of fidelity, and with the supernatural discernment that springs much more surely from your fatherly love than from your religious experience, you will discover those qualities of Jesus which correspond to your children's instinctive expectancy—or, rather, their divine preparation. One such characteristic is his infinite power over bodies and souls, a restrained power that seeks only to foster goodness. Then there is his kindliness, his friendliness toward ordinary people, who work for a living, marry, fall sick or die; and his graciousness toward the crowds that besiege him on every side, following him, shouting and pushing one another as the apostles try to silence or drive them away. Or his uncompromising crusade against the powerful and the hypocritical to insure justice for the weak and the oppressed. Or, again, his fearless fidelity to his mission, his dignity despite outrage, his love of nature, his affection for his friends and his zeal for his Father.

In particular, make your children see how human Jesus was and how much closer he actually is to them than they suspect. Convince them that, in order to resemble him, they need not cramp their personality but expand it. Prove to them that their spiritual life is so shallow, not because they spend too little time in church or at prayer, but because they are not more generous, more compassionate, more wholesomely ambitious, more perceptive—in a word, more human.

Lastly, teach them to find God in his saints and, here below, in every man who completes the manifestation of Christ and reenacts his passion. Tell them how meaningful, mysterious and thrilling life becomes when, behind each of the poor, we can discern Christ and, behind each event, divine providence. Train them to recognize Jesus in the breaking of the bread and, thereby, to grow more sensitive to all his other presences. Kindle in them a passion for saving the world—a magnificent enterprise in which faith predicts and interprets for us whatever will happen, and we, nevertheless, continually tend to lose heart and become terrified. "So stay awake, because you do not know when the master of the house is coming, evening, midnight, cockcrow, dawn; if he comes unexpectedly, he must not find you asleep. And what I say to you I say to all: Stay awake!"

Sacrifice

Children are naturally generous. Lest we reinforce this happy tendency by questionable means, however, we have to respect an essential hierarchy. Christian education is, first and foremost, an introduction to God's love for mankind: what matters is not so much what we do for him as what he does for us; the whole of the Christian religion consists, not in our having loved him, but in his having loved us first.

There is nothing more dangerous than wanting to rival God's generosity before we have understood it. There is nothing more pharisaical than wanting to be worthy of his love before we admit that he loved us even when we were unworthy. If we lose sight of this truth, we very soon consider God as one who receives instead of one who bestows, as one who takes instead of one who enables us to give. Thus we usurp his place and puff ourselves up into something bigger and better than the deity we invented. When the thought of God occurs to us, either we apprehend the sacrifices he requires and, therefore, do our utmost not to think of him, or we concentrate on our sacrifices rather than his blessings and gradually develop, in relation to him, the mentality of grudging benefactors.

Children are bookkeepers by nature, jurists, practical and naively self-interested businessmen. If imbued with the wrong spirit, they will sedulously fill in their "sacrifice scorecards" and accumulate merit without progressing in true generosity or, especially, in the love of God.

Surely, love cannot express itself or grow strong without sacrifice; but even more surely, sacrifice cannot exist or be fruitful without love. The entire process resembles a spiral whose starting point is, not a human, but a divine initiative. Only after we have pondered and marveled at God's infinite goodness toward us can it win us over and persuade us to start imitating it.

Religion in Adolescence

When your children reach adolescence, your role in their religious formation should become more discreet. At this stage, they flaunt their independence in all spheres and are quick to take offense: imposing a practice or a regulation on them suffices to make it contemptible in their eyes. As a consequence, wield your authority only in the essential matter of Sunday Mass; but remember that having to oblige them to attend means you have failed and must now adopt another method, as I suggested above.

The proper regime for adolescence consists in freedom which you sustain, guide and motivate. For instance, make bedtime such that you can all rise early in the morning; when scheduling breakfast on vacation, favor those who were with you (I hope) at Mass. Pray more if they pray less, and in your prayers ask for the patience and joy that will someday make them want to resemble people who pray.

Lighten your task by introducing your sons to whole-souled priests and interesting pursuits. Though a younger child should stay with his family, an adolescent cannot be kept in an incubator. On the contrary, send him out into an ever-widening but handpicked circle of friends and acquaintances, so that he may benefit from all the contacts, the experience and the responsibilities which homelife cannot offer him. But do not, for all that, surrender your office to educators from outside. Rather, cooperate closely with priest, scoutmaster and teacher in order to help your child derive maximum profit from all these influences and thereby strengthen his personality.

Be particularly careful to broaden your religious views and improve your way of presenting them. Just as you previously insisted on prayers at stated times, correct posture, and little acts of generosity and devotion to Jesus and Mary, so now make your teenager enthusiastic about a very human ideal: becoming a man, a gentleman, a hero, a leader. Avoid whatever could cause him to confuse the spiritual life with practices of piety (which often bore him). Teach him to appraise people and religious values according as they feed and radiate the vital flame of courage, generosity, perseverance and devotedness. Show him that, from a human standpoint, religion is something sublime which inculcates profound truths about our nature, allows us to judge ourselves rightly, and, above all, fashions a race of men who are more courageous, more loving and more lovable than all others. Then he will see that, instead of paralyzing him, you are helping him grow; instead of smothering him, you are letting him breathe in great drafts of invigorating air.

In point of fact, at fourteen or so, he suffers principally from religious indigestion and must be fed wisely. Usually he has no spiritual life simply because he has no ideal. His mediocre work, his mediocre ambitions, his mediocre reading and friends do not utilize—let alone absorb—even his natural powers. What, then, can you expect him to do with supernatural ones? Accordingly, the best method of leading adolescents to God is, first, giving them a lofty human ideal which will so whet their appetite that they will have to summon up all their resources and will personally feel the need of a few religious practices.

More important yet, if you have succeeded in this, if the ideal you have presented is high enough and their responsibilities heavy enough, they will learn an indispensable lesson: that man is radically weak and can never accomplish all he intends. Then, provided you have prayed well and prepared them fittingly, they will meet Christ. In their anguish they will call to him and confess, "I can't stand being so second-rate, so unstable, so enigmatic, so incapable of living up to my better self. Come into my soul and do what I can't: live in me the generous and noble life I helplessly aspire to." At that moment—like many other people before them, and like us if we have been blessed—they will see the power of God and learn to recognize him by what he achieves in them; they will discover from experience that faith actually does move mountains, that for God the impossible is a routine matter, and that Christ effectuates in them everything they despaired of doing.

With time, they will learn a still greater lesson: God delivers us not so much from our vices as from ourselves, and the only way to be freed from our pride, egoism and inertia is to be freed from self eventually by Another, who becomes more alive within us than we are.

Happy are the parents who, as discreet confidants or merely as loving witnesses, assist at their child's individual meeting with Christ. By allowing his distinctive spiritual personality to take shape alongside theirs, they prove how delicate their religious sense is and they instill in him a truth far more important than any dogma, any sacrament and any ritual—namely, that everybody has to discover religion anew for himself, that no one has a monopoly on it, and that this youngster should not have judged it by the way he and those around him lived it, since it is something entirely different, much greater, much more beautiful and beneficent. Happy, too, are the parents who know that religion is the realm where they must remain forever young, grow more and more child-like and continue to learn. In so doing, they will realize that none of us have understood anything yet, that we always fall infinitely short of what there is to understand, and that religion, therefore, constitutes the hearth where we become brothers and sisters to those whom we are training, where we commune in a perpetual search, and often make our most wonderful discoveries while observing and listening to the children entrusted to us.

By dint of imitating us, they excel us; and the singular reward of Christian parents and educators consists in noticing that a given child, though he tried solely to resemble us, grew to resemble Another, whose features we did not dare think we mirrored so faithfully.

IV
Study Habits

Poor Morale

Students are the most dispirited tribe on earth. Sabotage may present a problem in factories, but nowhere do we find more laziness, more indifference or distaste for work than in school, where the pupils rejoice when a teacher stays out sick or forgets to assign a quiz, where they scamp their tasks, apply the brakes on a course, and cheat and lie in order to avoid exertion or punishment.

In every class there runs a hidden but steady current of insubordination and rebellion. Most pupils study unwillingly and offer incredible resistance to learning. For example, they can take four years of Latin and succeed in not knowing their syntax, despite countless classes and drills, simply because they aim only at passing the next recitation and utterly refuse to understand, absorb and retain the material or acquire some measure of proficiency.

Parents and teachers are so accustomed to this attitude that it no longer disturbs them. Yet it should, for it causes a child to be unhappy throughout his years in school, botch his studies, or at least not benefit from them as he should—and this at the very age when he is most open to enthusiasm, brimming with good spirits and energy.

And unless he is interested, what can we honestly expect of him, since intellectual work cannot be forced from outside, can be estimated only with difficulty, and, in the long run, always permits a pupil's cleverness in shirking effort to outdo the teacher's ingenuity in spurring him on.

Causes and Effects

Of all the factors contributing to such a chaos, the student himself is perhaps the least blameworthy. Part of the responsibility lies with curricula which attempt to interest him in so many areas that he has no time to study even one in depth or taste the joys of research, discovery and creation; and with subjects taught in such a way that they speak to him of the past without fostering, enlightening and maturing his natural interest in the present. Part of the responsibility, again, lies with teachers who do not know how to hold his attention or how to make him do his share of the work instead of doing it all themselves, who exercise his memory more than his judgment, impose their views rather than elicit his, and would not dare sacrifice the theoretical program for the real one—for what can enrich him.

But as this book is primarily for parents, let us discuss their responsibilities. First comes the matter of guidance. Many a youngster suffers because his parents' ambitions exceed his potential. He is provided with tutors and force-fed on special courses; intermittently, he may even work; he repeats a year or transfers to another school, but always with the same results. (Today, guidance services offer counsel which, when corroborated by his teachers' considered opinion, can save such a pupil.) Secondly, assuming that this orientation has been handled properly, parents are duty-bound to keep encouraging, sustaining and advising their child.

Academically, the typical schoolboy's worst fault is fitfulness, which results from his being so easily and so frequently discouraged. For one thing, his studies are difficult, and the hydra-headed problems he encounters day after day weary and demoralize him. To write one word in a Latin composition correctly, he must recall half a dozen different items: the exact term, the spelling of it, declension, gender, number, rule or exception. He cogitates, avoids four or five pitfalls but stumbles into the sixth and rates zero for that word just as if he had never tried. The requirements of efficiency rarely allow a teacher to reward effort. For another thing, the student's goal is too remote. When, during our classical course, did we experience the joy of culture and thrill to literary beauty? Bricklayers are lucky: with each trowelful, they see results and, at night, can contemplate their day's work; but intellectuals know only in ten or twenty years that they have done something useful today.

Which of us would want to become a schoolchild and go through examinations again? To tell the truth, if we toil now, it is because we find our work interesting or at least remunerative, not because we are actuated by all the motives we propound to our children. That is why they need us so badly: we can encourage them because we have gone through the same ordeal and are now enjoying the reward which, as yet, they can only take on faith.

Beyond question, we have to reprimand and punish them, analyze their report cards attentively, and balance blame and praise. Everyone knows that punishing a child hurts the parents more than him, but this is no reason for them to neglect their duty. Years ago, in the school where I am, we arrived at a conclusion that astounds and sometimes angers parents when they are told of it: that, sooner or later, their child attaches the very same importance to his work as they sincerely do. We observed, for example, that when a sixty-five average entitled a boy to go home over the weekend, the vast majority attained sixty-five; and that when stricter and more discerning policy-makers raised the requirement to seventy-five, just as many students, after a period of wavering and wobbling, gained the ten additional points. But, of course, there is much more to it than that.

Study Habits

Though the educator's ideal is to help his pupils less and less until they can get along without him, still a definite amount and kind of aid is indispensable at the beginning of elementary- and secondary-school studies. It should consist in checking on methods rather than results, and unraveling difficulties by making children realize what a word means (something they too often overlook), by staging, illustrating or somehow concretizing the problem under consideration—in brief, by imparting sound study habits.

Parents constantly complain, "My son doesn't know how to work. Couldn't you teach him study habits?" That is precisely what a teacher does every day in class: he shows his pupils how to think and work; but what they are looking for is a technique that eliminates effort.

There is none. The only method lies in paying attention, using one's mind, thinking and comprehending. Like too many of us adults, however, the ordinary student detests that and seems to have no greater desire than to indulge in the delights of mental sloth: doing what he has always done, clinging to his own ways, putting difficulties off till later or shutting his eyes to them altogether.

The very order which a lazy pupil follows in working gives him away. He starts by doing whatever punishments he may have, recopies items from his notebooks, and then dashes off a task without bothering to make a rough draft. Lastly, if there is any time left, he studies his lessons. In other words, he postpones the moment of exertion as long as possible; he uses all his wits to avoid thinking.

Unwillingness To Think

Here is the archenemy of intellectual achievement at any level —this dread of brainwork, this idiotic wish to escape enlightenment. Our representative pupil guesses without checking, translates without construing or justifying, and amasses without evaluating, just as we gulp down a purgative to keep from tasting it. He throws raw beefsteaks into the stomach of his memory without troubling to cook, chew or assimilate them; at the next quiz, he will regurgitate them, startlingly similar and undigested, and then forget them totally. Persuaded that thinking is a waste of time, he wants immediate and reassuring contact with the material to be memorized, and believes he can learn better and faster if he does not take pains to understand.

We must explain to him that reading and studying are not passive operations but, rather, a kind of invention. Take, for example, a theorem in geometry. Merely reading it gets me nowhere. I have to reconstitute the reasoning behind it in my own mind. The illustration in my textbook and the notes on my scratch pad serve simply to direct or confirm my hypotheses. They are only signposts, and all their efficacy lies in the thoroughness of my investigation.

Likewise, reading an ordinary text intelligently is not a matter of spelling words, deciphering sentences and then rising to the thoughts set forth. Quite the contrary. Experimental psychology has proved that we read, not words, but only a few characteristic downstrokes which enable us to determine whether invention, after being launched by the opening idea, is still traveling in the right direction. In truth, to read is to create. We suppose, we guess intensely what the author is going to say, and we verify it by observing that the words in our mind agree substantially with those on the printed page. What matters is the vigor and power we bring to the internal task of invention, comprehension and verification: that sagacious blend is what makes us remember.

Memorizing

Most pupils, on the contrary, are associationists, heirs of a now discarded psychological theory which maintained that the simultaneous presence of two words in our consciousness forged such a link between them that the presence of one automatically evoked the other. The psychologist's whole task consisted in calculating how many simultaneous presences were required in order to memorize something. He would call on cooperative subjects, who went to his laboratory, read a text a certain number of times, and were later questioned on what they had retained. One day, however, a student who had volunteered and had read his text twenty times over declared he could not repeat any of it. The psychologist was nonplussed, and the student explained, "Nobody told me I had to remember anything." Experimental psychology has established that, in order to memorize something, we must want to.

A large number of us believe that we should know a passage by heart provided we have read it often enough. Conscientiously, therefore, we apply it to our mind like successive coats of varnish but do not, for all that, succeed in connecting and fusing the elements to be retained.

Practically speaking, there is only one way to learn: forever pausing to ascertain whether we understand what we have just read, and whether we can repeat it—preferably in our own words. There is only one way to judge whether we have read with the intensity required for memorization: questioning ourselves, at the end of each line and each paragraph, on what we have just finished reading.

Short of that, it is pointless to continue. A pupil of mine once said, "In first year Latin, I used to read a lesson twenty times and still didn't know it well. Now, I read it only once but take twenty minutes to do so, weighing each word, getting the idea, and seeing how it's related to what precedes and what follows. That burns up calories but it's effective. Even if I forget, I can always piece the lesson together again."

Furthermore, no one can claim he knows his subject matter until he has tested himself in writing, for he will very often be quizzed that way, and chirographic memory differs from oral memory.

Basically, studying is exciting because it is active. If pupils are bored by it, there is only one explanation: they are not doing anything; instead of focusing their attention on verities, they let it wander back to themselves. Those who truly study testify that using their mind is not that painful—certainly not as disagreeable as loafing and thinking about the work one should be doing. I pity pupils who dream instead of studying, who cannot stop thinking vaguely about themselves, their pleasures or their cares, and never advert to reality. Completely preoccupied with self-centered visions, they refuse to cast aside the warm blanket of revery in order to enter upon real life, which is simple and active.

Like love, work is a giving of self. It is love made visible.

The Right Use of Time

Draw up a system for your children to follow in doing their schoolwork. First, they should study the lesson on which their task is based, and then review the exercises done to prepare it in class.

This apparent waste of time proves extraordinarily fecund if students can ever be persuaded to try it.

Limit the time allotted to study. Your son needs rest; otherwise, he will work longer and longer hours and reap poorer and poorer results. Taking too much time for study is laziness, for it means increasing the length of effort so as to diminish the strength of it. His work load will triple and quadruple, but his work hours will not. The only solution is to force him to work faster by rationing his time—so many minutes for his task and so many for each lesson—and goading him to keep trimming a few seconds from his record as he races against the stopwatch like the track stars he so admires.

I shall not insist here on the need of creating an atmosphere that facilitates study: a peaceful existence, sober distractions (to avoid the multiplicity of interests which constitutes the high schooler's special kind of overwork), and cultural activities lived and enjoyed as a family, for a child retains best what he absorbs unconsciously.

Patience is a decisive factor in education. Let us be willing to adopt his rhythm before imposing ours on him, and admit that some pupils develop more slowly than others and take twice as long—even an extra year—to assimilate the same material. Unwarranted impatience on our part bespeaks selfishness and lack of understanding.

Above all, we should have quiet chats with each child of ours, where we can exchange confidences with him, listen to his fears and gripes, and compare our life experience with his in order to complete his (once it has been understood) by means of ours, which becomes acceptable to him the moment he recognizes it as something analogous and fraternal.

How long has it been since your last man-to-man talk with your son? Did you lash out against him or think his problems out with him? An adolescent needs moral support and advice, but he is too proud to accept them unless we treat him as an equal and remember the time and trouble we ourselves had to expend on becoming adults.

Let us be courageous and contagious optimists. As educators, in fact, hope is our foremost virtue. We must never lose faith in a child's future—even if he has no academic future—but allow him to lean on our trust and our love. For many years he cannot count on anyone else.

Ideals

In conclusion, every student needs an ideal. Do you recall the parable of the stonecutters? In a quarry, a sullen, disgruntled workman was making stone chips fly. When visitors asked, "What are you doing?" he would snap, "What does it look like? I'm hewing stone." His neighbor was doing the same job, but looked radiantly happy. To those who asked about his work he answered, "I'm building a cathedral." And a third man, earnest and luminous, declared, "I'm saving the world." All three were working at the selfsame task, but what a difference their outlook made!

Describe to your child the joy of being useful someday, of living a worthwhile life and meriting to serve his fellowmen. If you want to slake the thirst in his soul, extend this concept of service immediately to the communion of saints. Before he will bother enlightening himself, he needs no less of an ideal than illuminating the world. He must kindle a fire that can warm the whole earth, before he will agree to come and sit, like the first of his poor, near the hearth which he has built solely for others.

Improving oneself means improving the world. To our children, generous as they are, this truism offers the most compelling motive for self-enrichment. Once they believe that their own suffering can lessen universal suffering proportionately, once they see the purpose of pain, they find the courage to bear it as though it were nothing.

Read them this magnificent passage from Léon Bloy: "Our freedom is correlated with the equilibrium of the world. Whenever we perform a free act, we project our personality unto infinity. If we give a penny to a pauper grudgingly, it pierces his hand, falls, bores its way through the earth, rives the sun, rips across the firmament and compromises the universe. If we commit an impure act, we cloud perhaps thousands of hearts whom we may not know but who communicate with us mysteriously and need that we be pure, just as a parched wayfarer needs the glass of water mentioned in the Gospels. A charitable deed, an act of genuine compassion sings God's praises in our name, from Adam down till the end of time; it heals the sick, consoles the despondent, calms tempests, redeems captives, converts infidels and protects mankind."

This is the bread our children hunger for: a bread of heroism and holiness. At the age of twelve, they all yearn to be missionaries and save the world. Now is the time to remind them that no one ever saved the world except by discharging the duties of his state in life, and that the most effectual means of aiding the destitute and championing the weak, evangelizing unbelievers and sustaining martyrs, is to buckle down to work with all these intentions in mind.

Recently, as often happens at the beginning of a school year, one of our pupils began to lose heart at the sight of the unfamiliar difficulties that were cropping up. The headmaster met with the boy's parents and teachers, and suddenly one of them had an inspiration: "I'm going to make him coach a classmate who's even slower than he." The result was a complete transformation. While helping another, he both forgot and outdid himself. With the generosity characteristic of their age, young people will do far more for someone else than for themselves; and, in the process of encouraging a weaker comrade to bear up under problems and pressure, they disregard their own fears and troubles. As the saying goes, "You made me stronger by leaning on me."

V
Reading

"Come on, Peter, close that book. We're all at table waiting for you." Peter slides off the sofa, still reading, his inscrutable face wrapped in a sort of fervid torpor. Like a blind man, he shuffles along slowly, brushing past end table and hassock, riveted on his book till the very last second; reluctantly, he perches it on the edge of the buffet, faceup and ready to resume, without losing a moment, after the parenthesis called dinner. Then he sits down. At first, his head droops, still dizzy from the rush of pleasure and haunted by the last impressions sown in him, which seem to sprout and bloom as if suddenly released by this interruption. For a minute, he remains motionless, then lifts a blissful face, peers at the family quizzically, laughs as though surprised to find them there again looking the same as ever, bids a last farewell to his dreams and joins in the conversation.

The Dangers of Reading

Picture a child hypnotized by his storybook, an adolescent spellbound by a novel, or a nonchalant commuter who dozes off whenever the murders in the latest whodunit let up a bit. Do you think there is any use talking to them about the art of reading, about making this pastime or passion of theirs an open door to culture? For eighty percent of the boys who indulge in reading, it is anything but an art, a discipline, a means of self-enrichment. Rather, it represents a dark craving for solitude, a voluptuous and vertiginous descent toward annihilation, and a frenzied ecstasy of escapism. For others, it means a superficial diversion, either a titillation or a soporific, to which they consistently prefer the repetitious but

67

sociable joys of conversation or the exhilarating pleasures of games and sports.

Education through reading is an onerous and frustrating task. Only with difficulty can you foster a love of books in someone who has no taste for them; if you succeed, on the other hand, you unchain demons who will prove twice as hard to master.

When you consider the dangers and abuses occasioned by reading, as well as the slight benefit derived from most of it, you may sometimes wonder whether the reading habit is necessary or whether play, conversation and conventional studies suffice for normal development.

Why should all this dreaming, this adventure, this escape be indispensable to the formation of character? Must personality, in order to grow strong, regularly faint? For, surely, most reading entails losing consciousness, not to mention wasting time and repudiating one's own life to live that of others. Reading has often been defined as a dialogue between the reader and the author. But none of our children dialogue that way; they monologue feverishly (like grown-ups) and never abandon the *I* of conscious life and current conversation except to capitulate entirely before the author and empathize with everything the hero of his story thinks, says and does.

If a young person hopes to discover a congenial image of himself by bending in every direction writers and producers suggest, he may very well break his back; and if he surrenders to each and every influence, he will most likely lose the strength and independence which he needs in order to select and cultivate the right one. His sensitivity will turn into a sponge that can absorb everything but cannot react, and his weakened personality will unquestioningly obey the promptings whispered to him by uncontrolled memories. Thousands of young people, constantly attitudinizing and encumbered with fictitious personalities, can no longer distinguish their real self from all the characters they have slavishly accepted to be through their reading and viewing.

At this point, you are most probably thinking, "Now that he has denounced reading, he feels obliged to say a few kind words about it." As a matter of fact, I would gladly have deleted this preamble

if I did not find a description of the psychology of the young reading public essential to understanding the art of reading. Once we
know what our children do and what they look for as they read,
we can counsel them more pertinently and convince them more
easily.

Speed

Let us admit from the start that excessive, hasty and haphazard
reading numbs the mind without nourishing it, dizzies and intoxi-
cates it like a whirlwind tour, which does not really multiply the
number of impressions received but merely jumbles them all together. "Do you want to learn how to read?" asked Faguet. "Read
slowly at first; then read even more slowly; and afterwards, down
to the last book which you will honor with your attention, always
read very slowly."

That is a most unpalatable piece of advice for a generation of
young moviegoers accustomed to watching twenty-four images flick
past per second; for this jet-age breed, crazed by distractions, fads
and upheavals, and persuaded that their unconscious is the surest
refuge from today's problems.

Authors themselves are partly to blame for cursory reading. So
many books and magazines flood the market every week that either
we must follow Monsieur Pouget's advice and read only such
works as deserve to be learned by heart; or, if we want to keep
abreast of the times and not risk missing—I shall not say a masterpiece—but a fertile idea, an original viewpoint or a precious source
of information, we must race through everything that reaches us
(more or less weeded out by the comments of friends and review-
ers) and schedule frequent and thoughtful rereadings of the rare
beauties hidden in that hodgepodge.

Children should be encouraged to reread. Most of them do so by
themselves, and their enjoyment and fidelity to the practice indicate
that this is their real reading. Without turning a mere technique into
a hard-and-fast rule, I always advise a pupil to underscore the best
passages in every worthwhile book and then reread them at leisure,
with the full understanding that presupposes a knowledge of the

complete work, and in the reflective mood that cannot dawn until his curiosity has been satisfied. I am afraid we have to resign ourselves to the fact that modern youngsters will truly relish only what they reread.

The Advantages of Reading

Although we have pegged precipitant reading as a form of the contemporary flight into the unconscious, we must not conclude that reading in itself is a flight, an escape. Quite the opposite. If you want to seek escape from reality, if you want to observe living unreality, look at the life most grown-ups lead—a drab, petty existence which they hold up to every child as a model of realism. But he refuses to believe them if he has other lights and infallible instincts. Disappointed in his teachers, he turns to books; misunderstood by his elders, he gets along famously with great minds. A child's most precious asset is his inherent faith in the nobility of man, in beauty, excellence, the sublime meaning of life, the tragic and mysterious character of destiny. To develop into an unshakable and operative conviction, this faith requires a world of books —books of adventure, travel and war, as well as love stories, biographies, philosophy and all the poetry that can pervade that broad range of works.

Let us not forget that such a "romantic" conception of life comes straight from the Gospels and that all other books must serve only to prelude or shed light on the prodigious love story of God and man. No less a teacher than God has told us of the fearless daring ("The violent are taking [the kingdom of heaven] by storm"), the enthusiasm (". . . no one who looks back is fit . . .") and the vigilance ("Stay awake!") necessary in any walk of life; the incredible adventure in store for us, to the astonishment of good and bad alike ("Lord, when did we see you hungry or thirsty, a stranger or naked, sick or in prison . . . ?"); and the infinite value of the briefest moment in the lowliest existence. No life is richer, more eventful or exciting that the life of faith—that journey in search of God, that attentive gaze which, in everything, perceives divine plans to be furthered and souls to be saved. Crushed as we are by the merest nothing and always straining toward trifles, we can hardly give our children a sufficiently exalted and stirring idea of their destiny. Consequently, we had better help them find it in the company of heroes, poets and saints.

Practically speaking, then, reading is the best way for young people to explore the outside world in its true dimensions of time and space, but chiefly to discover their own inner universe and glimpse the men they can become by living the life, not only of the heroes they love, but especially of the author. Sharing his vision of the world and sensing his faith and attitude, they will be influenced not so much by the subject treated as by the man who treats it. That is why we must spurn mediocre works, even though at first sight they seem to moralize more than works of art.

Furthermore, the distinctive pleasure attached to reading lies in the fact that it is done in solitude—in the solitude which we moderns dread and avoid, and which humanism, says Mounier, must teach us both to understand and to endure.

But the reader's solitude is a populated one, a perfect spiritual communication which leads man to his greatest depth but does not abandon him there defenseless. For Mounier, experiencing solitude means growing conscious of the whole nonspiritualized fringe of our interior life. Now, reading spiritualizes that interior life, thereby nourishing solitude and making it bearable. With their perennial challenges, books constantly summon our flabby minds to intellectual activity. Heedlessness and indolence prevent us from descending voluntarily into the depths of our being, for we shrink from the dismal solitude that reigns there. Reading, however, draws us into what Proust called a "populous solitude."

Thus, reading cures the illness which it causes. A means of escape into the unconscious, it is nevertheless a most potent remedy for fear of the conscious; it teaches us to bear with ourselves by feeding our interior life with the spiritual marrow of great men.

"Still," someone may object, "in the intellectual and the moral order, nothing comes easy: it all has to be earned—the hard way. This is no place either for annuitants or for beggars, who live solely off the work of others. How, then, can reading be so beneficial? At any rate, wouldn't some program of personal reflection or meditation do even better?"

The answer is simple if we stop for a minute and think of this: we are never more completely ourselves than when we are introduced into ourselves by another—an artist, a writer or a saint. We are never in fuller possession of our powers, never more open, more receptive and active, more understanding and critical, than at the supreme moment when admiration for a work of art, the magic spell of style, or the revelation effected by prayer or religious ceremonies has liberated us from our sterile superficiality, our distractedness and agitation, our narrow, utilitarian views. At last, we can think as we have always wanted to think, love as we have longed to love, and express ideas to ourselves as we would have liked to express them in the first place.

In the bosom of our solitude (which reading respects and fosters), in this prompt and happy exercise of solid abilities that tend to retract and vanish when someone else steps in, our mind tests itself and, sooner or later, is justifiably amazed at the mastery and joy with which it functions.

We should then multiply these blissful ecstasies in which we continue to travel, alone but unaware, the skyward road that reading has opened up to us. Always reassured by the nearness of our guide, and nourished and sustained exactly when and as necessary, we can boldly climb toward the heights. Eventually, declining help and relying on our own strength, we strike out on new paths before the wondering eyes of our teachers. And there on the summit, we create that unique song which no one could whisper to us and which we could not compose alone, but which our books taught us at the very instant we ceased hearing them.

It should be clearer now why the deadliest enemy of reading is the impetuous speed that winds our mind, overtaxes and bewilders it without ever giving it free scope. Earlier I emphasized the difficulties of combating haste; here I wish to add a few words on preventing it. When your children are still very young, read them the loveliest verses and stories, those that are charged with meaning and evocative power. For this—the age of tales and rhymes, of trust and docility—is when you can train your youngsters to breathe to the exquisite rhythm of inspiration-action, image-thought, reality-dream and poetry-prayer. Once stabilized by the wholesome habit you have transmitted to them, and once captivated by the beauty of these intervals, they will not, on their first solitary contact with books, behave like famished savages who plunder and devour everything in sight.

Let us, therefore, start our children along the road to reading, however perilous it may seem. This is an adventure on which they must all set out; and the mere fact of walking—because it compels them to inhale deeply, dries the mire on their shoes and sends the blood coursing through their veins—will itself repair the accidents it causes.

All we can do is select specific dangers and proportion them to each child's age, humbly remembering that such calculations are hazardous and that, if devils break loose, we shall soon be overpowered.

It is our duty to counterbalance the influence of books by the thorough upbringing we provide. As a result, even when a child no longer accepts us as mentors, the tastes, inclinations, principles and behavior patterns which we have inculcated in him will join forces, from deep within his nature, to fight the battles we cannot wage personally. Preparation for reading goes hand in hand with preparation for life, and neither form of training can be successful without the other.

What To Read

Which books should we start with, and which reserve for later in the educational process?

As I have already noted, we cannot be too careful in choosing the first ones, those that we read aloud to a child and that offer him a foretaste of literary pleasure. Here I would place the Gospels (excerpted and adapted, of course, but retaining a goodly number of characteristic and evocative expressions); then verse chronicles,

Grimm's Fairy Tales, poems from *A Child's Garden of Verses* by Robert Louis Stevenson, a few of Aesop's fables, and some episodes from the *Iliad* and the *Odyssey.*

Such readings by a mother to her child will etch ineffaceable memories in him. An inflection of hers, a word or an allusion will help him to understand; familial warmth and affection will stimulate emotional response; and everything will become more beautiful, more significant for having been learned and loved together. And we teachers shall no longer encounter those miserable young dunces with empty heads, stagnant imaginations, and cruelly constricted hearts which can only suffer because they have never learned to love.

Healthy, vivacious, outdoor children rarely love reading. It puts them to sleep. Again, they have to be introduced to this new world when they are still very young. To whet their interest, tell them only the beginning of a story; then leave the book where they can finish it for themselves. In the backyard or in their own puppet theater, let them reenact highlights from *Robinson Crusoe, The Swiss Family Robinson* or Jules Verne's *The Mysterious Island.*

If necessary, try a few "Illustrated Classics" so that the pictures may induce your children to read the text. But choose with care and only as a last resort, for their imagination, once catered to by the illustrator, can no longer be aroused by the writer; and a charming style (if such a thing exists in publications of that type) is wasted on minds that have already been cloyed.

By the same token, preserve your youngsters from shallow, flashy picture magazines, which are as detrimental to true reading as the movies are to deliberate concentration. From early childhood, so feed their mind and imagination on noble adventures, generous ambitions and glowing memories, that they can no longer tolerate the mediocre and the ready-made but demand texts which allow them to dream and find themselves again.

Among the books which I would pass on to my children, I distinguish two major categories or currents.

The first comprises adventure and ideals, a copious and vivifying stream where adventure gradually decreases and ideals emerge purer and sharper.

I would start with tales of chivalry such as the *Song of Roland* and some of the Arthurian legends, *The Scarlet Pimpernel* by Baroness Orczy, the five volumes of "Leatherstocking Tales" by James Fenimore Cooper, and *The Jungle Books, Kim* and *Puck of Pook's Hill* by Rudyard Kipling.

After that I would continue with the adventures of heroes of the air (*The Spirit of St. Louis, We* and *Of Flight and Life* by Charles A. Lindbergh) and the sea (*Fight of the Firecrest* and *In Quest of the Sun* by Alain Gerbault), of polar explorers like Scott, Byrd, Amundsen and Charcot, of alpinists (*Last Crevasse, Mont Blanc and the Seven Valleys* by Roger Frison-Roche; *Challenge of the Unknown, No Latitude for Error* and *Schoolhouse in the Clouds* by Sir Edmund Hillary), of underground explorers (*More Years Under the Earth* by Norbert Casteret), and of saints (*The Perfect Joy of Saint Francis* by Felix Timmermans; *Saint Francis of Assisi* by G. K. Chesterton; *The Secret of the Curé of Ars* and *The Secret of St. John Bosco* by Henri Ghéon). Next would come adaptations of the bible and biographies of Jesus (as, for example, those by Dickens and François Mauriac).

And I would end with the poets: Paul Claudel (*Coronal*), Charles Péguy (*God Speaks*), Francis Thompson, Gerard Manley Hopkins, Rabindranath Tagore, Kahlil Gibran and all the others.

Nor would I forget the masters of imagination and humor, like Antoine de Saint-Exupéry (*The Little Prince*), G. K. Chesterton, Mark Twain, Dickens (especially *Pickwick Papers*) and Alphonse Daudet (*Tartarin of Tarascon* and *Tartarin on the Alps*).

The other category comprises observation, accounts of experiments, and knowledge of the world around us.

Here, besides such standard works as *Insect Adventures* and *Insect World* by Henri Fabre, there are excellent young people's encyclopedias on birds, insects, minerals and the like.[1] Much information of this sort can be gleaned from fiction like *Bambi* by Felix Salten or *The Call of the Wild* and *White Fang* by Jack

[1] American equivalents of the works which the author lists here would seem to be, for younger children, "The Golden Nature Guides" and, for more mature ones, "Life World Library," "Life Nature Library" and "Life Science Library"—Tr.

London. Jules Verne is basic: a child who has not read him will be ignorant, perhaps for life, of the principles behind all modern inventions and, consequently, will fail to understand our civilization. He must learn the laws of aerodynamics in *Five Weeks in a Balloon,* of submarine travel in *Twenty Thousand Leagues Under the Sea,* water displacement by ships in *A Floating City,* astronomy in *From the Earth to the Moon* and *All Around the Moon,* and every human endeavor in Verne's masterpiece, *The Mysterious Island.*

The War of the Worlds by H. G. Wells and *Lord of the World* by Robert Hugh Benson will make a youngster ponder the living conditions of mankind now and in the future.

From there I would go on to history and geography, novelized biography and travel books.

And finally I would come to man, to the study of the most diverse and complex being on earth. Younger children can gain insight into themselves and their peers from the stories of Father Finn, "The Hardy Boys" series, and more mature novels. But from about the age of sixteen on, they should become acquainted with the queen of sciences—psychology—through works like those in the following brief list:

Joseph Conrad: *Typhoon, The Nigger of the Narcissus, Lord Jim, Youth, Victory, Heart of Darkness.*

Antoine de Saint-Exupéry: *Airman's Odyssey, Night Flight, Wisdom of the Sands.*

Ivan Turgenev: *Fathers and Sons* and the short story "First Love."

Honoré de Balzac: *Eugénie Grandet.*

Henry James: *The Turn of the Screw* and *Daisy Miller.*

A. J. Cronin: *The Citadel, The Keys of the Kingdom, The Green Years.*

Paul Bourget: *The Night Cometh, A Divorce.*

Dale Carnegie: *How to Win Friends and Influence People.*

Graham Greene: *The Power and the Glory, The Heart of the Matter, The End of the Affair.*

Lytton Strachey: *Queen Victoria.*

André Maurois: *Disraeli.*

Romain Rolland: *Beethoven the Creator, Michelangelo.*

Hervé Bazin: *In the Name of the Son.*
Georges Bernanos: *The Diary of a Country Priest.*
Albert Camus: *The Plague.*
François Mauriac: *The Vipers' Tangle, The Woman of the Pharisees.*
Feodor Dostoevsky: *Crime and Punishment, The Idiot, The Brothers Karamazov, The Possessed.*
Charles Morgan: *The Fountain, Sparkenbrooke.*
Julien Green: *Diary, 1928–1957.*
Jean-Paul Sartre: *The Words.*

Even then, many gaps remain to be filled before an adolescent acquires a solid literary background: among other things, he ought to study monographs on the arts, read widely in numerous areas and peruse the classics.

Incidentally, it seems that parents should be able to rely on a boy's teachers to promote love of the classics, since these are the works that are studied in school. Studied? Yes, perhaps; but largely left unread. To correct the situation, we must insist on and convince teen-agers of this extremely beneficial rule: "Read a book while you are actually studying it in class, while people are talking to you about it, or when you need it." We ourselves all did the opposite: we devoured the latest novels while seeing the classics, and enjoyed the classics only later when our literature courses treated of contemporary authors. Let us try to persuade the coming generation to read—no, not Caesar, of course—but the *Iliad,* the *Odyssey,* Xenophon's *Memorabilia,* Plato, the *Aeneid, Tristan and Isolde,* Shakespeare and so on, when the professor is explaining them or, better still, a little before, lest his learned philological introduction or the mere cover of the classroom text generate repugnance.

"Furthermore," we should warn them, "don't read everything that comes your way. You retain something from a book only if you have preconceived notions about it to be confirmed or refuted, or if it ties in with your present preoccupations." Now, there is one excellent means to guarantee that: always having some project, some piece of research under way and, consequently, four or five books waiting to be read—a strong safeguard against the inane, superficial, pointless reading urged on us by every form of modern propaganda.

So far, I have said nothing about detective stories. It is impossible to express the scorn they deserve and the harm they do to real reading. If we have understood the nature and the benefits of literary enjoyment, we can see how incompatible it is with those breathless, bewildering narratives that clamor to be read at one stretch and, when finished, have not renewed our conception of life, our knowledge of man or our vision of the universe, but have kept us in a futile spin for two hours. Even on their own level as mathematical or psychological problems, such tales discourage reflection, since the reader, accustomed to being tricked by the author, no longer pauses to work out a solution for himself when he can get it easier and sooner by reading faster.

Introduce your children to reading, therefore, to real reading. For friends, give them the greatest men of all time; for ideals, the sublimest adventures; and for horizons, the whole world. But be especially careful to provide a home that will not disappoint them when they return to it, exhilarated and inspired by their climb to the heights. Lastly, teach them this priceless truth: that the most beautiful work of art a man can produce is his own life, and that he can expend so much love, intelligence and faith on his everyday duties that they become the noblest and most heroic adventure of all.

VI
Adolescents on Vacation

"Vacation time at last!" shout the children. "Vacation time already?" groan the parents. "Vacation time—unfortunately," sigh the teachers for several weeks after school reopens.

Still, we can perhaps conciliate these views by analyzing the problem they point to and planning vacation time at least as carefully as we plan other important occupations.

The parents of older children often face summer with apprehension, with a feeling of inadequacy and helplessness which these teeners do anything but dispel. "That's when they slip away from us," runs the familiar complaint. "But how can we possibly hold on to them? Isn't it better to let them do as they please than spoil their vacation and ours with endless bickering? After all, we go away to rest! And, anyhow, it doesn't seem worth crossing the children during these few days: they'll be scolded enough at home and at school." The fact is that joining battle with them and resisting the erosion they so expertly effect by their cajolery, their sulks, their disregard or their schemes, takes a degree of strength, endurance and courage which many parents lack.

Yet the cause of education is one and indivisible: you must not destroy today what you built yesterday. A child's vacations, like the rest of his life, should be educative. Though there may be a holiday from his textbooks, there is none from serviceableness and courtesy, much less from the state of grace. Sunday Mass is not discontinued for July and August, and you must make sure that he attends and keeps in top spiritual form by confessing, communicating and praying. As the Count de Vogüe remarked, how-

79

ever much we misevaluate an idea, it remains self-consistent and sweeps us along to its logical conclusion. When a weak-kneed educator attempts to purchase peace with total concessions, he soon learns that such a peace costs more than war. And unless wise but fixed rules spell out a child's religious, individual and family duties, the vacation period will end with incessant recriminations, mutual discontent and, sometimes, moral catastrophes.

Unfortunately, we are not inclined to impose such rules. In child training, there seems to be a law of alternance, according to which a strong-willed, rigorous, domineering generation is regularly succeeded by a liberal, permissive one. If a person had stern parents and was raised in fear, submissiveness and frugality, he very often conceives one paramount ambition: to spare his children the restrictions from which he suffered. Then again, precisely because he was well brought up, he is more mellow, humane and equanimous, and his children profit from the happy results of the educational principles which formed him and which he disallows today. Conversely, and for identical reasons, a person who was given too much comfort and latitude often treats his own children far more severely, far more imperiously and intolerantly than his parents ever treated him.

If this "law" were true, one would have to conclude that the present generation of parents was . . . very well brought up, and that the next runs the same risk, but that this in-between one is benefiting excessively from the amenity, indulgence and broadmindedness of its parents.

In general, parents do not realize how badly even an older child needs them or how much influence they still exert on him though he seems to be closing up and rebelling. They have trouble believing in something as natural as the love of a child and the incomparable power it gives them over him. If only you could guess how deeply your children love you! They do not always show it, but they are bound to you by their very essence; no one else holds the same ascendancy over them or issues the same challenge. Because they feel solidarized with you and sense how profoundly you can sway them, they sometimes react against you more violently than they would against anyone else; and that is the proof—painful but sure—of your action upon them.

During adolescence particularly, they rarely display affection, no longer coax, and only briefly allow themselves to be spontaneous. Still, their love is not diminishing but only seeking better ways of expressing itself. And meanwhile, till the new, adult manifestations have been worked out, your teen-agers act all the more timid and sensitive as this need obsesses them and cannot be shaken off.

Vacation time is ideal for exercising parental influence and establishing beneficial contacts between yourselves and your children. Accordingly, you should reserve a major part of your vacation for family life. With teen-agers, I suggest dividing vacation time into three segments: the first, for the entire family; the second, for some form of service; and the third, for individual vacations.

The Family Vacation

As the summer months draw near, it becomes increasingly obvious that parents and children hardly ever see eye-to-eye on how to enjoy leisure. There are two kinds of vacations and, unfortunately, they are incompatible. Grown-ups want relaxation and comfort, lounging, hotels and motor trips, whereas young people look forward to playing games, running up and down, building and reconnoitering. One kind rules out the other: parents either drag their children off to adult diversions or sacrifice their own desire for idleness, ease and luxury to the youngsters' need for activity, Herculean tasks and roughing it. (For that reason, I sincerely hope parents can get away by themselves for a few days of real rest, but not as part of the family vacation.)

A normal adolescent craves activity and adventure. He comes home with a thousand projects, a thousand dreams and plans, and usually wants to run back out as soon as possible. In his mind, vacations are for hustle-bustle, hard play and exploring; he rests by doing everything he cannot do while school is in session. By and large, parents take the opposite view: for them—and this is understandable, considering their hectic and exhausting life—vacations are for resting at last, and they rest by doing nothing.

Perhaps that is the main reason why parents and children cannot understand one another: they have nothing to do together. If friendship and love consist not so much in being with one another as in doing something together, and not so much in looking at one another as in looking together in the same direction, we have to conclude that a family lacks unity because it lacks common activities and purposes. Too many parents feel worn out by daily living and, in their weariness, shrink from effort and excitement. Another adult can sympathize and excuse them, but no child will forgive them. He needs young-minded, strong-willed, enterprising parents to imitate now and later in life. Otherwise, he reacts in one of two ways: either he inherits and redoubles their defects, becoming still more apathetic, skeptical and existentialist than his parents; or he simply escapes from this depressing atmosphere as they sigh: "He's always gone out."

Some parents cannot imagine why a child, after having been raised according to all the wisest principles and given only the best example, will, at a certain age, drift away from them and behave scandalously. The reason is that they never shared a goal or built anything together with him, and always endeavored to spare him any trouble instead of having him shoulder his part of the work and difficulties. Why does so many a teen-ager look passive, blasé and hard-boiled? Why is he erratic, mulish, spineless and incapable of getting up early or denying himself anything, although his parents are hard workers? Possibly because they have concentrated on turning their home into a relaxation area for themselves rather than making it the center of family life for him.

The right environment for an adolescent is one where people are doing something. He needs a home life that affords him the joy of helping to create family spirit, the stimulation of having piles of projects to look ahead to and unlimited opportunities for cooperation. He needs parents who take a lively interest in everything, who can pass sound judgment wherever he is concerned, and provide sure guidance in choosing from among everything which the modern world offers pell-mell in the line of fashion, reading, films, radio and television broadcasts, modes of living and vacation amusements.

Only parents with solid convictions and a firm character, as well as the ability to think and judge and react, can survive this stage without feeling overpowered and yielding to the day's rank permissiveness. Because they themselves are alive, because they feel younger than their child, and because they offer him so much that is worthwhile, they can exact a great deal from him in return and refuse him many things. In a word, they have the courage to be strict.

A few words now about planning the family vacation, which presents problems when there are children of widely different ages and tastes clamoring to be heard.

The seashore is not advisable except for young children. Older ones find it monotonous, since there are few places worth visiting and all the amusements are expensive. Besides, it tends to disperse the family and enervate the teeners in it, who wander about aimlessly with chance acquaintances. The ideal would be the mountains, a cottage in the country or even a campsite.

Whatever you choose, avoid the kind and degree of comfort which exempts you all from working, improvising and adjusting. Instead, let your children sense that they are shaping their own life and contriving to make you and themselves cozy. They should feel that you need them. The more there is to do, the better; and if the maid has come along, everyone ought to pitch in and help her so that she, too, may rest a little.

Beyond guaranteeing that all keep busy, you still have one essential precaution to take. If you admit—and you should—that most families are too limited to ensure the full development of their teen-age members, make a point of finding collaborators and surrounding your own family with a circle of congenial young friends. Vacation-time activities can be delightful or dull, depending mainly on who is present. Group a few families—relatives or friends—around yourselves, and invite your sons' and daughters' best friends to join you. You will have to choose carefully; but see to it, if you want to hold on to your adolescents, that your family milieu includes both boys and girls.

On the principle that preventive measures are always better than repressive ones, you can afford to be exacting about a youngster's choice of friends only when you yourselves have found some for him. Moreover, if you keep your welcome mat out, you can expect to put up with noise, confusion and fatigue, and to expose your children to some indiscriminate mingling, which is always dangerous but much less so than chance meetings and clandestine relationships.

It is natural and vitally important for boys and girls to meet and be in one another's company, and there is no more favorable place than within the family circle. Of course, you cannot content yourselves with issuing invitations and then vanishing discreetly "so as not to cramp the young people." On the contrary, you should mix with them, diffusing good cheer, inspiring novel ideas, games or projects, and setting a level of conversation and demeanor which they would not attain unaided.

This socializing between boys and girls, however, is wholesome only if the intrinsic interest of the occupations that bring them together outweighs the interest generated by their reciprocal attraction. Instead of looking at each other, they should all look toward some mutual achievement and learn to see one another without becoming hypnotized. The group ought to stay together, united in their common enterprise, rather than break up into isolated couples. Family life and the presence of well-balanced, energetic adults can abundantly supply this interest which liberates the young and helps them overcome their nervousness in the presence of the opposite sex. Thus, the friendship between them will bestow on everything they do together unparalleled zest, joy and dignity.

To conclude this section, let me offer several suggestions concerning your schedule and activities.

Draw up a sufficiently broad but regular daily program, which, among other items, should include a decent time for rising—early enough to go to Mass now and then. The whole morning is wasted if you start by lazing around. Therefore, invent tactful ways of getting everyone to say "Good-night" at such an hour that you can all rise bright and early.

With a little imagination, you can think up all sorts of jobs, excursions, games and championships to start the ball rolling, figuratively as well as literally. Dull and sluggish as children often are when left to themselves, they will overflow with vigor and enthusiasm if given the needed impetus and atmosphere.

Damming a stream, digging a pool, building a play gym or cabanas, exploring caves, observing the local wildlife at daybreak or nightfall, collecting something, doing a bit of botany or entomology, making wicker baskets and weaving, not to mention cleaning out the attic or weeding the garden, painting and puttying the window frames, reading a book for eventual group discussion, competing in indoor and outdoor sports, learning songs, studying guitar or flute—all this your children will tackle with gusto if they can work or play in pleasant company, if you know how to spark them, and if you shrewdly ask their opinion and cooperation instead of imposing chores on them. It does no good to ask patronizingly, "How can you stay there for hours without doing anything? At your age, I kept busy by myself." Go further and develop the art of involving them, almost without their knowing it, in enterprises which you select and they enjoy. And be sufficiently young at heart to play with them—cops and robbers, if nothing else.

Vacations and Service

Because adolescents must learn not to live only for themselves and their pleasures, part of their vacation should be devoted to thinking of other people and affording a vacation to those who could not otherwise take one. Older children can serve in neighborhood programs for the underprivileged, baby-sit free of charge, entertain in homes for the retarded or the aged, or work in the Negro and Indian missions of the South.

This will come about quite naturally since, during the family vacation, you have already taught them to render service by organizing games and modest celebrations, shepherding idle children, helping a farmer get his hay in, singing at Mass or assisting the celebrant worthily as altar boys.

Individual Vacations

It is obvious that the teeners' individual vacations also need to be planned and realized with parental guidance. Training in personal responsibility is necessary but must be gradual. With trustworthy companions, young adolescents can make a one- or two-day jaunt now and then, and older ones should be allowed an occasional longer trip once they have gained experience and proved themselves. It is unsound never to extend confidence, but naive to extend total confidence. You have to counsel, sustain, control and encourage.

Foreign travel is now in vogue. Most teen-agers who go abroad, however, learn nothing and have unpleasant experiences besides. Learning presupposes a foundation and especially a degree of attention and perseverance rarely found in youngsters on holiday. Furthermore, some parents do not realize how vulnerable and influenceable an adolescent is, especially when out of his milieu. Choosing a reliable family for him to stay with is difficult. Not many of us would care to be responsible for a young foreign visitor, since performing the task conscientiously would spoil our vacation. So, too, with the families that take your child in: few will look after him as they should.

Study tours are even more dangerous. If parents knew what goes on there, they would often be horrified; still, the fact that their child is in Mexico or England or Switzerland seems to anesthetize their imagination, as though everything must be fine in a country so different from their own. They know their compatriots well enough to be distrustful, but they have utter confidence in anyone a thousand miles off. Actually, no teen-ager should be sent abroad unless he is mature enough to judge and absorb the good he sees without jeopardizing what he has learned at home.

At this point, it might be well to mention conditional exams. Preparing for one should take no more than two weeks of intensive study, and your children are better off to repeat a year than forgo most of their vacation to attend summer school. For one thing, they would cleverly manage to catch up on their rest during the first trimester; for another, they could not assimilate in two months what they failed to grasp in ten; and for a third, they would only impair their health and trail the class again all year.

You may protest that there is nothing very reposeful about planning this kind of vacation. Quite right. If anything, you will come back feeling that you have worked, organized and spent yourselves more than you do the rest of the year.

But your children will come back wonderstruck, and their dearest memory of the whole vacation will consist in this: that they saw you as they had never seen you before—so much closer to them, so much younger and more stimulating than you can ever look during those long stretches when the daily grind monopolizes you.

As for yourselves, you will feel, if not rested, at least rejuvenated and renewed. Your children will have done you good; you will know them better and be able to guide them more easily; and you will be prouder of being their father and mother.

I have known families for whom vacation time was absolutely the best part of the year. "While we're on vacation," the children in a large family told me, "Mother and Dad belong to us. They give the maid a leave of absence, and sometimes we even pull the shades down so the neighbors will think we're gone and not come ringing the bell. Then, happy just to be alone together, we work and play and enjoy ourselves."

One couple, who had four sons of different ages, had become so adroit in handling them that, when vacation time neared, they asked, "What are your plans, boys?" (An adolescent rarely knows what he wants, but one thing he always knows: that he does not want what you would like to force on him.) Then, without directly excluding them but without inviting them either, the father quietly announced, "Your mother and I are going to take that trip we've been talking about lately." The boys would have objected to any attempt to cart them along, for, having been well-trained, they had plans of their own for traveling and camping. If the parents had insisted on a family vacation, there would have been general disagreement as to time, place and activities. But now, on hearing

them talk about going alone, the boys felt forsaken and almost instinctively thought what only the youngest dared to ask aloud:
"How about us? Can't we go with you?" Familial diplomacy had
triumphed and, somehow, despite their busy vacation schedule, they
all found time to spend a couple of weeks with their parents.

Part II
AT SCHOOL

VII
Today's Child

The Spirit of the Times

The case of today's child is being tried in every court, every book and film, but especially in every family: "In my day, we didn't do this. . . . We wouldn't have said that. . . . We never took such liberties!"

Though raising children has never been easy, we have to admit that it is more complicated now than ever before; but we must also assert categorically that the responsibility for this situation does not lie with today's child. According to most biologists, he is born identical with the children of a thousand years ago. At birth he is neither more nor less perfect than we were at that moment; in fact, his chromosomes and genes—that is, his hereditary factors—come from us. How, then, can he be so radically different? The only explanation is in the quality of the educators who molded us and the quality of those who have molded him and now keep reproaching him. The seed was the same, but everything depended on the atmosphere in which it grew.

"Oh, yes," you may protest, "I know what you're leading up to. Like all those other modern educators, you blame the parents. In a minute, you'll be telling us that there are no problem children but only problem parents, and that bad children always come from bad homes."

No, that is hardly what I had in mind, for, despite everything, I do not believe that the parents are most to be censured. What is sick today is not the children—and not even their parents—so much as the times in which we are living. Ours is an epoch without faith, so that universal doubt has become the common creed; with-

out security, so that we are always on the brink of war or the
eve of the Flood; and without optimism, so that we see only
anguished faces and hear only prophets of doom. But in order to
grow, young people need faith, security and optimism above all
else. Much as you, within your own family, may repulse the tidal
waves of contemporary feeling and opinion, still you cannot protect
your children against all infiltration from outside or against the
influence of companions who have been less well guarded.

Psychological Repercussions

Today's child, even though he comes from a close-knit family
and an excellent environment, bears the marks of modern life and
is invariably described as nervous, distracted and incapable of
concentrating.

First, he is nervous. He lives only vicariously through his parents,
in tempo with this whirling, pounding jet age. He loves violent
emotion, and his favorite diversion is reading James Bond epics,
watching gangster movies, and attending motorcycle or auto races.
Besides that, he is soft and, consequently, all the more nervous.
Shielded from physical unpleasantness and moral coercion, he has
never learned to suffer, to wait, to resist a desire or achieve self-
mastery. As a result, he cannot endure the least delay or vexation
and he rejects every form of constraint, including politeness. This
weakness of character gives free play to his instincts and nerves.

He is also distracted. When he applies for admission to our
school or any other, his character certificate generally boils down
to this: "A very gifted child, intelligent, curious, likeable, but extremely volatile and unable to focus his attention on any subject.
Forgets everything. Has no system or study habits." The explanation is simple: radio and incessant noises have taught him not to
listen anymore; speed, movies and television have accustomed him
to not seeing; and endless distractions have made concentration
irksome. He lacks curiosity—or, rather, vigorous and purposeful
curiosity—because omnipresent sounds, images and gratifications
have irresistibly lured him away from pursuits that require intellect
and perseverance.

Bluntly, he is incapable of paying attention. You can repeat the same thing a hundred times; and if he finally hears you, he looks surprised, as though you had never mentioned it before. Well may you complain, "There's no use telling him anything: I might as well be talking to myself. What ever made him this way?" For a partial answer, consider how many years the radio has been blaring now—without his listening to it—through every meal, every conversation and every homework session. Teachers who have him in class will be obliged to put him through long silence therapy in order to clear his head of reverberating sounds. Short of that, he must remain deaf. For additional answers, consider movies and speed, which have made him blind as well. Used to seeing twenty-four pictures per second, he has lost the habit of observation; and racing down the highway at seventy miles an hour, he cannot study nature but only watch the road if he is old enough to drive or the speedometer if he is too young.

Not only is his attention engrossed or, at best, divided, but it is also too short-lived to produce anything solid. He has seen or heard about everything yet knows nothing accurately, for, when still very young, he developed the habit of letting himself be bombarded by ideas and sensations without taking time to fix them in his mind. Claudel explains: "The cinema, which sweeps over us, wave upon wave; the automobile, which turns nature into a sort of colored wind, and jazz—everything is designed to produce a sense impression which is supplanted by other sense impressions at the precise moment when it was about to transform itself into thought. As soon as the image is born, it dies."

By way of contrast, listen to what Robert d'Harcourt says of Goethe's education: "The principal method used to amplify his intellectual endowments was observation, truthfulness, limpidity and a steady gaze at the object being studied. . . . [This resulted in] the inestimable asset which we may call 'sharpness of impression.' " To acquire something of that sharpness, twentieth-century children would need a whole reeducation—such as hearing a melody and then being obliged to repeat it, or examining a picture and then drawing it from memory or at least describing it in detail. A person learns how to learn before he is six and before he ever sets foot inside a classroom. (Sometimes a teacher from our school is assigned to a rural area. There, in some peaceful little village, he finds, to his astonishment, pupils who retain everything they are told because they engrave it deep in their mind. The experience soon teaches him to stop despising his former dunces, those poor city children who would be just as capable if their environment had not prepared them so poorly for the learning process.)

Lastly, today's child is passive. Since I have already discussed this point in several connections, I shall not belabor it here but simply state that the whole emphasis nowadays is on comfort and away from effort.

As a case in point, take the use of machines and gadgets. Our civilization tries, wherever feasible, to replace human labor by mechanical power. Yet, if a child matures through effort—and that is an incontrovertible fact—these modern machines, by dispensing him from effort, also dispense him from maturing. Man is a being who creates himself. The weakest of animals at first, he rises superior to the others only by means of his conquests, which are made possible because, when he is young, his curiosity, his need for activity and his zest for the new and unknown are boundless. In her prudence, nature had inflicted on passivity the unbearable penalty of boredom. This day and age, unfortunately, has discovered how to camp before a television set, stare at a motion-picture screen or ride around in a car, doing absolutely nothing and still not feeling bored: it has invented instant pleasure and ready-made thrills, which enable man to forget the boredom that would otherwise motivate him to improve his character and keep wholesomely busy.

An Attempt at Reeducation

Our school, whose organization and methods I shall describe briefly in the next three chapters, uses every means at its disposal to react against this debilitating influence.

We established ourselves out in the country, since fresh air, broad horizons and a great deal of play and sleep can cure nervous children. Seeing our pupils come to life again on the playing fields and recreation areas amply demonstrates the immense benefit they derive from this relaxation.

We want our pupils to put their heart and soul into what they are doing. Consequently, we start by ascertaining each boy's deepest interest and then using it, whatever it is, to stimulate him. Despite all statements to the contrary, the prime reason for academic failure is that some pupils do not *want* to learn: they go to class resolved to do as little as possible, and they retire into lethargic hibernation so as to protect themselves from anyone who would force them to work. Both in and out of the classroom, we strive above all to waken these sleepwalkers, to recharge these quitters and interest these idlers in their personal life, so that they may truly live—right here at school—instead of just dreaming about past or future weekends. Our courses and teaching methods are lively. During class periods, which are kept moving with questions and laughter and the spirit of emulation, we make the students work hard, investigate and think hard. You may be surprised to hear that our boys, though they have an hour of sports every day, also have six hours of class and two to four hours of study. We borrow extensively from the findings of modern pedagogy in order to obtain, with techniques adapted to the mentality of today's children, the same results which older pedagogic systems obtained by different means.

As I shall demonstrate in the following pages, our educational methods are based on three principles. First, we propose to show our pupils that happiness does not depend on money, gadgets or luxurious surroundings, but that it springs spontaneously from their ingenuity and mutual understanding and that by fully utilizing each man's resources they can transform their class, their scout troop or club into an industrious and joyful little city, enriched with all the potential discovered in each of its members.

We also try to foster great warmth and confidence between our students and ourselves. Diderot once exclaimed, "What do you expect me to teach this lad? He doesn't like me!" The average child—even in his late teens—will not learn to love his studies unless he loves his teachers: his mind unlocks and opens wide only if sympathy has turned the key.

Lastly, we appeal to our pupils' generosity in all circumstances. For example, we entrust younger boys to the care of an older one, certain that he will do far more for them than he would for himself. In every conceivable way, we see to it that our students help us; for we want them to become more and more actively involved in everything we do for them, so that someday they may be perfectly capable of replacing and surpassing us.

VIII
A New
Educational Method

I convoked the teachers in my schools and said to them, "Make no mistake about it: I have entrusted the children of men to you, not that I might eventually weigh the sum total of their knowledge, but that I might rejoice in the manner in which they have climbed. I am not interested in a pupil who sees a thousand mountaintops while he is being carried about in a litter. . . . I am interested solely in that pupil who has exercised his muscles by actually scaling a mountain—even one. . . . When I say *mountain*, I mean *mountain* for you who have bled on its brambles, rolled down its precipices, sweated on its crags, culled its flowers and breathed the bracing air on its summit. But when I say *mountain* to some fat storekeeper, the word conveys nothing to his heart."

—Antoine de Saint-Exupéry: *Citadelle*

A New Method

We believe it is necessary to renew educational methods and to keep renewing them constantly. Educators must always observe the child, study him, sound him and adjust themselves to him in order to adjust him more effectually to us and to his future role. Just as the world unceasingly evolves and just as the child is always new, so should education evolve and always be new. With time, even the truest principles become false unless they are adapted; and, at every turn, we realize that the moment someone says something absolutely true, he has said something new.

Therefore, we "follow" our pupils intently—so that we may lead them, once we have understood them. We continually remold discipline, environment and cadres, and improvise means of educing from each boy all the capabilities which he possesses but, so often, keeps concealed. Far from rejecting tradition, we listen to our predecessors, we consult the experts and study the psychologists; but it is precisely their teaching which preserves us from dogmatism, and their example which rescues us from routine and placid adherence to what we have always done.

Many judicious parents study a child, detect and satisfy his needs, foresee his reactions, treat him tactfully and adapt their disciplinary ideas, their exigencies and even their character so that they may help him develop to the full. We have resolved to continue their policy, and, therefore, we loudly proclaim: "We shall do the same as you have done—love your children and gain insight into them. For us, also, there are no two alike; and we are prepared to change all our ways, all our procedures and all our sanctions if we see that your children need it." That is our best method.

A Living School

Monitors fear lively, boisterous pupils. At our school, we fear only the passive, the uncommunicative. Gently, we try to reach those who come to us ill-trained: the deaf, to whom one can repeat a rule of grammar or discipline fifty times without their grasping, remembering or even hearing it; the inert, who understood all too well that they were being asked only to keep quiet; or the frivolous, in whom long hours of class and study have developed nothing but a prodigious capacity to amuse themselves with trifles. What these sleepyheads need is competitive sports, swimming, the strict discipline of teamwork, quick-paced and quick-witted classes, active and challenging companionship. They have to find out that they can "live" though at school, and that benefiting from our guidance and our courses calls for every ounce of their youthful vigor and strength and gaiety—in short, for everything which they imagined they had to put aside the day classes began.

In our opinion, we are dealing with a generation that is both extremely sluggish and extremely restless. Keyed-up and irresolute, these boys have just enough energy to drag themselves from an easy occupation to a passive diversion. Long-range efforts discourage them. Considering the age at which they come here, we feel that the most salutary treatment for them is twofold: stimulating them to activity by means of very brisk courses, emphasis on initiative and responsibility, together with varied sports and interests; and, at the same time, calming their nerves by means of fresh air, well-organized relaxation, absolute silence throughout the school at certain hours of the day, and firm discipline which the vast majority of our students not only accept but even desire.

Residence Halls in the Country

It is a crime to open a boarding school in the city. However, if circumstances do not permit otherwise, the classroom building might be located there, but the residence halls should always be out in the country. Bussing the students in for class each morning is better than immuring them twice—in a city and in a dormitory.

We have noticed that our boarders are happier in proportion as their dorm is farther from their classes and looks less institutional and more homelike. Indeed, the first requisite for relaxation is a total change of atmosphere from the classroom building to the residence halls.

In view of this, it is imperative to break the usual monobloc into a series of residences, each sequestered in a green grove. Every trip to or from brings us back to the heart of nature: thus, on our way to the central dining area, we have sunshine or rain, wind, flowers and trees to cheer and renew us. Gone are the long corridors with their cobweb tapestries; gone also the plodding herds of acquiescent pupils, the noisy refectory and those immense study halls with proctors ready to pounce right and left.

Crowds are ineducable. To train them, you must first divide them. Each residence here houses thirty to sixty pupils, a group small enough for all its members to know one another. Not only is the program adapted to their age and needs, but the students themselves draw it up. They feel at home in their hall and assume the responsibility of decorating and maintaining it; they are active members of an articulate and independent group which has its own regulations, leaders and traditions but, especially, its pride and team spirit.

Vertical and Horizontal Grouping

Our pupils are divided according to age (level of development, that is, not chronological age), and in two different ways: the youngest into homogeneous groups comprising ages seven to ten and ten to twelve, and the rest into several parallel vertical groups from twelve to eighteen.

Needless to say, the educative atmosphere is enriched by the contribution of more varied personalities and becomes almost familylike. The seriousness of the older boys quells the turbulence and prods the insouciance of the younger ones, whose cheerfulness, enthusiasm and winning ways in turn shake the inertia and bring out the devotion of their elders.

In the main, upperclassmen tend to underachieve. Because they are completing one phase of their education, they feel they "have it made" and simply coast along. Being responsible for a younger group, however, and transmitting to it what they themselves have received incites them to give better example. Similarly, teaching newcomers to respect a rule becomes one more reason to keep observing it. Then, the spirit of our school—to interest pupils in their formation and that of their companions—develops in these older boys, who become staunch witnesses to it. The end result is an influential elite that commands attention because of an undeniable difference in age and maturity. They uphold the traditions of the group in which they live for three or four years; and, if these master spirits are choice enough, the president of the group can ultimately exercise the apostolate of a chaplain in his residence hall, gaining in ascendancy whatever he can delegate in authority.

A School for Difficult Boys

"Keep this up, and we'll send you off to boarding school!" That is how we get our pupils.

Boys are rarely easy to manage; and those who are, it would seem, are rarely the best.

The need for independence which grieves you mothers and vexes you fathers is nevertheless a sign and a promise of the strong personality which your child will someday have. No doubt, the manifestations of it are often disconcertingly rude, stupid and negative, but you must not make the mistake of battling the cause itself along with awkward expressions of it. When he rebels against purely external constraints, he is simply showing his mettle, though you somehow conclude that you have lost your influence over him.

Not at all! This teen-ager, who seems stubborn when you lock horns with him, is sensitive to ideas, readily imagines that he himself has discovered the very ones you suggested to him, and ardently defends yours against an outsider right after contradicting them in front of you. More sentimental than he would ever admit, he loves you when you are not around to know it, and has to fight back his tears if angry; he yearns to be consoled for having behaved so badly, and needs only a gentle word from you to melt the armor which he donned so that he could parry your power. He despises and maltreats himself, goes numb with despair, and is perpetually swayed by his moods, his friends, public opinion, the weather, you and everything. If you could see all this as clearly as we teachers sometimes can, you would no longer find him unmanageable. Like us, you would hear in each of his defiant shouts a strangled cry for help; you would run to shore up his feeble strength, his unsteady independence; you would protect him from yourselves and everyone else, and, while feigning to talk with the man he pretends to be, you would discreetly suggest satisfactory ways of asserting and fulfilling himself.

In truth, he is too vulnerable to be treated with anything less than infinite patience, encouragement and respect. Before any adolescent, we parents and teachers must be self-effacing, gain acceptance as witnesses instead of imposing ourselves as masters, promote the emergence of this personality which challenges ours, and conciliate it to ourselves even in the measures we take to curb its excesses.

"A man had two sons. He went and said to the first, 'My boy, you go and work in the vineyard today.' He answered 'I will not go,' but afterwards thought better of it and went. The man then went and said the same thing to the second, who answered, 'Certainly, sir,' but did not go. Which of the two did the father's will?"

The whole drama of adolescence is compressed into this parable. There is no need of long commentaries on the "docile" child, his "mother's darling," the jellyfish who agrees to everything and questions nothing, but who thereby betrays his shallowness and his weakness, that lamentable dependence which will prevent him from ever growing up.

But do you understand the first boy and really prefer him? Did you recognize your son in that insolent "I will not go"? How very much you have to love this difficult child, tormented and buffeted by his need for independence! He is pessimistic and has a poor opinion of himself, for he knows his weak points and distrusts even his strong ones. He no longer dares give his word—perhaps because he once failed to keep it and is too conscientious to disappoint you again, or perhaps because you have bawled him out, repressed him and sapped his confidence by refusing to give him yours. But there is a much better explanation for his rebellion. Your son is too good, too loving and sensitive, too desirous of doing right and too inclined to yield to you. Sensing that this is bad, he decides that he must first say "No," declare himself independent and prove that his obedience does not spring from weakness, childishness or sentimentality; so that afterwards, liberated from himself and you, from his fear and his servile attachment, he may love you sincerely and obey you freely.

IX
The Honor
System

A Delicate Balance

The principles of this new educational method are evident: we must give a pupil all the freedom he can handle; furthermore, we must arouse and cultivate his need of and pride in independence, for it will prove to be the mainspring of his conduct.

Here is what I mean. Any sound upbringing begins with discipline, with the development of conditioned reflexes and absolute obedience, but should end with autonomy, personal conviction, and a sense of responsibility and cooperation. Our task as educators is to effect a successful transition from the first to the second of these stages.

A child is born with a weak will and strong instincts. Leaving him "free" would enslave him to his whims, whereas our rational authority liberates him by reinforcing his feeble will with our firmer will. When he obeys, he experiences the joy of doing what he ought and, at bottom, wants to do but would lack the courage to if left unaided.

The whole problem is to regulate our mediation according to his exact needs. If we interfere too much, we undermine his will by preventing him from using it: he acquires the habit of doing but not of wanting to. Thus, he degenerates into the classic boarder—a phlegmatic, snail-paced, eternally weary creature who arrives on Sunday as into a tunnel of bricks and cement, with his brains turned off and his emotions and spontaneity chloroformed, and goes back out on Saturday after having learned, given and suffered as little as possible. On the other hand, if we offer too little help, discipline no longer supports but crushes him: excessive responsibility makes his taut will snap.

We are not, therefore, compelled to choose between two antipodal methods—one based on authority, and the other on freedom. All child training begins with authority and very little initiative, and ends with initiative and responsibility and very little authority. In short, authority and freedom, discipline and initiative, should be the flexible, alternating components of all education properly understood. Yet the value of a pedagogic method lies far less in principles than in the fidelity, cleverness and perpetual invention with which they are applied.

What, practically speaking, is the honor system? Only its traditional adversaries and the profane still equate it with the absence of supervision. Actually, it is a little more complicated than that.

Honesty

The first duty of any educator who wants to place confidence in his pupils is to merit and gain theirs. Confidence is reciprocal: teacher and pupil both expect it from one another and strive to justify it. This emulation creates a climate of moral excellence without which there would be mere dupery, since we hardly care to deserve the confidence of those whom we judge unworthy of it. Consequently, our principal concern is to treat all our pupils, not with a show of trust, but with good sense, fairness and a clear policy that will win us their minds and hearts.

Now, educators, be they parents or teachers, are forever catching themselves in flagrant acts of hypocrisy. Children may tell fibs, but so do their elders—from evasive or fanciful explanations of sex and birth down to our empty threats, which are ill-considered, exaggerated and rarely executed anyhow. The average youngster hears countless lies at home and at school; so that when we trap him in a lie, we would do well to remember that "the son can do only what he sees the father [or the Reverend Father!] doing." The most common reason why our adolescents lose the faith is that they eventually see through adult phoniness.

We sometimes feign confidence when, in point of fact, we are counting only on our authority and supervision; or we pretend to trust the boys simply because we cannot be there to watch them or because any offense will add weight to our reproaches when we catch someone red-handed. But how many of us sincerely aim to enfranchise the young from our authority and to associate them step by step in the government of the family or the school?

There are two concepts of education between which to choose, though we too often implement both simultaneously in case one fails. Either we must legislate everything, supervise constantly, and thus dispense our pupils from thinking and willing; or we must require much by virtue of an exacting ideal, but command as little as possible, gradually letting them shoulder the responsibility for their own conduct, so that they may learn to get along without us. We should not plan their daily life for our convenience as proctors, but put ourselves at their service loyally to help them grow up to independence.

In fact, once their early training is over (training that some recruits, unfortunately, have skipped altogether), education consists in respecting their spiritual liberty (but not their caprices), in having them see obedience as something noble and desirable, and in making their nascent personalities our allies against their instinctive individualism.

Modern children, particularly, are unaccustomed to imperatives, and frequently come to us hardened by blundering coercion. Still, with their native generosity and the spur of an ideal, they can impose a rigorous discipline on themselves if we propound it manfully instead of trying to subject them to it by force.

The Honor System

As soon as a pupil enrolls in our school, especially if he has had enough experience to be able to compare, he is struck by the fact that it is manifestly organized "for the student": the professors are interested in him, the regulations are mere common sense, and the amusements and games are thought out as carefully as the courses. In his residence hall, he enters into a new atmosphere, which is entirely different from that of the classrooms and therefore facilitates relaxation and favors initiative. There, he is welcomed by friendly companions, who teach him the ropes, draft him for a team, and lure him into their favorite sports and clubs. He soon learns to distinguish a whole hierarchy of team leaders, group leaders, custodians, judges and courts, and gets acquainted with two teachers who live in his hall like older brothers and work on their own projects in the study, join a team on the playing field, and express their views at the weekly council. Instead of facing a monitor who both distracts and irritates him, the new pupil finds himself in the middle of a spirited and active group and has his hands full keeping up with it.

The hub and focus of such a group is the council, a meeting held once a week or oftener, where the regulations and interests of that particular group are set forth, explained, debated and, frequently, voted upon. Nothing creates a spirit as effectively as discussions when they are well conducted: a hundred difficulties are raised and ironed out which would otherwise have remained as permanent sources of secret dissatisfaction; interesting cases concerning discipline or study are cited, commented on and either held up as examples or submitted for general disapproval; the group's regulations and customs are periodically reexplained, perfected and modified as to practical details; and, meanwhile, each student can contribute his ideas and voice his agreement with others, thereby committing himself to uphold whatever the group decides. Hence, the teacher no longer defends these rules single-handedly but is seconded by the boys' personal convictions and the power of public opinion, which has ratified the measures and witnessed everyone's consent and, sometimes, individual promises.

The work of the council is completed by two agencies: the special committee and the court.

The team leaders form a committee which meets at least once a week, with or without the president of the group. Responsible for the smooth functioning of their team, and even of the group as a whole, they serve as intermediaries, presenting the pupils' wishes and grievances to the president, and inducing the pupils, after adequate explanation, to abide by the decisions which the authorities occasionally submit to the committee. The role of the team leaders expands as the groups grow older, and in the vertical groups (from twelve to eighteen years of age) their influence becomes preponderant: they preserve traditions, assume responsibilities, support new enterprises and govern their restless charges.

Finally, the court, when made possible by general agreement and the availability of a few tactful and influential students, gives a group autonomy and a strong sense of responsibility.

This court results from an agreement between the teachers and the pupils in any group, whereby we teachers place our disciplinary power, and the pupils place their obedience, in the hands of several older boys whom we have all voted to the bench. The pact runs for a month. At the end of that time, there is a review of the dispositions which the judges have made, an open discussion ending with a vote on whether the system should be continued, and the election of new judges or the reelection of the present slate.

The court's competence extends to all cases where the good of the group is at issue. Though the judges may convene on their own initiative or at the request of someone involved, they should step in as rarely as possible.

When the court operates well, it performs an inestimable service for a group. Educators everywhere deplore the fact that the good are almost always timid, if not downright cowardly, whereas the bad strut about brazenly and enjoy a sort of prestige. With a little maneuvering and hypocrisy, these undesirables often become leaders whose impunity disheartens and scandalizes many a better person and whose success seduces the weak. In this connection, our court constitutes a body which, by common consent, arms the good citizens of academe against those who behave unworthily, permits the serious-minded to assert themselves as they should and as everyone secretly wants them to, and, lastly, affords them a means of pressuring delinquents without having to resort to "the authorities"—in other words, without tattling.

Moreover, the boys come to realize that discipline exists for the well-being of the student body, not of the teachers, and that each pupil is therefore duty-bound to make himself responsible for it.

This solves the difficult problem of chastisement very neatly. What destroys a student's confidence in his teachers, causes him to contract the habit of lying, and perturbs and depresses him above all else is those unfortunate punishments, detentions and work details sometimes decreed in the heat of indignation with excessive severity and frequency.

Even when the court is not functioning, our disciplinary procedures lean toward mildness. We warn and urge for a long time before taking harsh steps; on occasion, we allow the culprit himself to decide how he should make amends, and, at the first sign of goodwill, we often cancel the penalty.

Before the judges, of course, it is harder to lie, since the pupils know one another too well. In general, they dread the judgment of the court more than that of a faculty member: for when a professor censures them, they can take comfort in indifferent or "anti-prof" public opinion; but when their peers condemn them, they have nowhere to turn and must necessarily face the facts. It follows that such trials are rare and become still rarer the longer this system has been in force.

As an extra protection, boys who distrust the judges may always ask to be subject to ordinary jurisdiction again—that is, to the authority of the teacher concerned. But no one ever requests this exemption, and the teachers are very glad because they feel that being able to depute their disciplinary powers leaves greater room for moral influence, and because nothing is more pleasant than living in a group which is so profoundly animated with their spirit that they need no longer have recourse to their authority.

As you can see, confidence is mutual. At first, I intended to discuss only the confidence which we try to merit from our pupils, but I have already been led into discussing that which we place in them. In the next chapter, I shall treat of this second point expressly and show how we teach them to deserve the same confidence we have asked of them.

X
Loyalty

Any true educator strives to inculcate in his pupils respect for the law, for the truth and for themselves. But we can rarely boast of having succeeded—especially in this anarchic period of history which spawns so many sharpers, frauds, gate-crashers and rebels that our adolescents are disinclined to play the game of life because everyone is cheating.

In this regard, schools are the worst place of all. Lying and cheating go on continually, a veneer of politeness covers ingrained hostility toward superiors, assiduity is ridiculed, and general rejoicing greets any disorder. Even the best students, though they disapprove, ride along faintheartedly and, by their inaction, become accomplices in the crowd's foolishness and cruelty. And yet we are dealing with the most generous and enthusiastic age group, the one that could best warm up to the ideal of loyalty.

From the start, however, we must recognize that very few pupils—extremely few—deserve our confidence. Not only has their childhood training failed to instill trustworthiness, but it has often taught them to close up within themselves, to dissimulate, and to scuttle, ever so passively and underhandedly, a group's efforts to reach unanimity or a class's resolve to study well. At the beginning of the year, we frequently have to launch a campaign against this "schoolboy mentality," against pupils who eagerly take advantage of the facilities here without giving their loyalty and devotion in return, and who pretend to respect the rule but are determined to violate it the moment no one is looking.

Granted that pupils do not inspire trust; still, we cannot withhold it from them. The disillusioned teacher who thinks himself cured of naiveté because he has lost faith in his students, never understood the honor system. He was mistaken in applying it and is now mistaken in refusing to. A true educator, on the other hand, realizes that he must grant confidence, not because the pupils deserve it, but in order that they may learn to deserve it someday. At our school, we extend confidence in advance, knowing that in this domain, as in many others, need arises before capacity. If a boy appreciates the reliance placed on him and strengthens his sense of honor, we rejoice because we have succeeded; and if he disappoints our hopes, we rejoice again because we have found a concrete way of helping him to feel how weak he is and how badly he still needs discipline, support and guidance.

Instead of watching closely (as in traditional boarding schools) lest any infraction occur, we deliberately leave the door open for minor failings and refuse to formulate laws so perfect that they would smother all initiative and preclude all wrongdoing. A group never functions better than after some breach of trust which enables us to make every member see the ugliness of disloyalty, the responsibility of all for the failings of one, and the need of constant vigilance to remedy and avoid doing harm.

If anything, an excessively tight rule imprisons the whole student population, good and bad, weak and strong, between a ceiling which is so low that the best are not inspired to rise, and a floor which is so solid that the worst do not dare tunnel a way out. They can all lie there together, passive and apathetic, and vegetate without incurring blame. Then, too, the proctor is always around to stop them in time.

Here, on the contrary, we give a boy as much latitude as possible so that he may reveal his inmost nature, and then we offer help according to his needs. A threadbare but nonetheless accurate comparison will illustrate what I mean. If you are teaching someone how to swim, you should not leave him utterly alone, for he will drown; but neither should you hold him so high that he cannot possibly choke, for then he will never learn. The secret is to keep giving him just a little more freedom than you know he can handle.

To put it another way, a poor educator is like an actor or an orator who mounts the rostrum and harangues vehemently before a classroom full of his pupils. Ensconced in their comfortable seats, they glance at him distractedly, with a blend of mockery and sympathy, agreeing one minute and yawning the next, sure of one thing only—that they want to get out. As their teacher, he should be sitting in the critic's seat, and they should be up there literally making a spectacle of themselves. From his modest and attentive position below, he could then give them encouragement and advice, a frown or a smile, and have them repeat until they learn.

Sincerity

First, let us dispel an erroneous idea of sincerity.

Our age prides itself on loving truth and hating formalism and conventions. But, too often, its sincerity is of the oratorical type, which consists in saying whatever one thinks and assenting to whatever one feels.

Heaven only knows how often I have heard today's teen-agers say, "Look, I've got to be sincere. I've got to admit that I'm lazy, that I like to see somebody get it in the neck, that I enjoy brooding, don't give a rap for most of my classmates, and sometimes hate the people I ought to like most. This is the real me, because it's the way I feel. So I'm not going to be a hypocrite and fake sublime sentiments. I'm what I am, and that's how I'll act."

To each of them I answer, "This is false sincerity. You're observing yourself like a fact, describing yourself like a thing. What seems to be honesty is a lie, for you're much better than you suppose and quite different from the person you've described to me. Proof is that you're dissatisfied, you're unhappy about the way you are, and you suffer from it. Genuine sincerity—the only kind I'm interested in—makes you search for your true self, rip off the countless masks that your ideas and emotions foist on you, perfect your character and rise above yourself till you become the person you are way down deep."

In the words of Louis Lavelle, the philosopher, "To be sincere is to reveal oneself in the process of self-improvement; it is not merely ascertaining facts about oneself, but doing something about them. Sincerity is an impulsion to be oneself, to create oneself." It does not consist primarily in introspection or psychoanalysis (such inventories of our nature would disclose that we can become anything), but it leads us to conform our life to our duty, to take our place in the world, and assume full responsibility for ourselves so that we may try to become what we should.

The pursuit of sincerity, then, is dynamic. It means believing that our ideal of self-transcendence is the most sincere element in our makeup, despite all the infirmities and humiliations that could dissuade us from admitting so.

We should explain to the young that any man, even though he has weaknesses, remains infinitely respectable as long as he remains sincere, because he dissociates himself from his weaknesses and denounces them instead of attempting to justify them. We can neither scorn nor condemn him, since, in his very lapses, he bears witness to the fundamental nobility of man: he continues to respect this ideal of transcendence and moves toward it while acknowledging that he has not attained it. If he lies, on the other hand, he repudiates this ideal, covers up his frailties and shields them from the one antidote we have; he sides with his misdeeds and elects to stay as he is rather than rise above himself by preferring that which he should become.

Truth is the air our personality breathes in order to grow, and falsehood is self-deception before anything else.

At first, lying proves difficult: the beginner blushes and gets confused and tangled up in his fabrications. To lie masterfully, he has to delude himself, disfigure and destroy himself. A real liar can no longer tell the truth; in fact, he reaches the point where he cannot even recognize it. He lies without wanting to and half believes his lies. For him, truth and falsity are one and the same. In the *Inferno,* Dante pictures liars as men without faces, unidentifiable persons who resemble no one and nothing.

Suppose you force a child to beg forgiveness. Suppose, too, that his honesty is intact, still undivided by the abyss that later separates what we say from what we think. He will refuse because, being so good and innocent, he knows that if he said the words and made the gestures, he would end up really begging forgiveness. By connaturality, he senses the value of loyalty. It is as precious as the enamel on our teeth, and our first lie does to our conscience what a cavity does in our mouth. Once the enamel has gone, all the brushes in the world are useless.

Lying to others means breaking off communications with them and locking ourselves up in solitude. For a while, this may give us a curious impression of power, since all of us—even as children —are strongly tempted to cut ourselves off, to excommunicate and damn ourselves. In our pride, we insist that we are self-sufficient, that we can ignore others and be happy alone. But we were made for communion: we subsist only through mutual contact, and anyone who would deprive others of his riches deprives himself of theirs.

Falsehood kills confidence, so that even the truth becomes doubtful. Yet, in the popular mind, the worst consequence is to be trapped in a lie. Accordingly, we entreat children, "Your personality is still fragile. Please don't burden it with the utter shame of being branded a liar." What we should do, rather, is remind them that telling the truth is a relief, an ineffable joy; and that punishment, if it must follow, is far more desirable and liberative than remorse.

Prerequisites

Surely, the principal cause of lying is cowardice: fear makes almost everyone disloyal. Nothing, says Lavelle, demands more courage than "to act, when we are alone, as if we were being seen by all, and, when we are seen by all, to act as if we were alone."

For this reason, we should prize independence of character and foster it in those whom we are training. Because both children and adolescents are highly impressionable, we must protect them from ourselves first, lest they be crushed by the strength of our personality, and them from themselves and their inordinate desire to please or oppose us.

Basically, there are two behavior patterns which denote excessive influenceability in a boy. First, he answers what he thinks you would like to hear, he adopts your ideas through affection rather than conviction, and he comports himself in a way calculated to gain your approval—all of which reveals a serious disregard for truth in him and in the parents or teachers who tolerate such a course of conduct.

We should propose models of independence to our young people through stories like that of Marshal Foch, for example. While still a student at the military academy, he acquitted himself so well during maneuvers one day that his side won the battle. The general who had judged the proceedings then met with the two leaders and immediately criticized Foch's adversary: "My friend, your problem is quite simple: you set out with a preconceived notion. Now, that is extremely poor strategy. You must base your judgment on facts, observe the terrain, counter the enemy's moves, and not hamstring yourself with theories." Next, he turned to Foch and said amiably, "And you, Commandant, tell us how you won this brilliant victory." "Well, General," answered Foch, "I had a preconceived notion. . . ."

Conversely, there is the story of the vaporizer. In order to teach his students the scientific spirit, a university professor called them into the auditorium and asked if they would cooperate in an experiment. "This vaporizer," he began, "contains an extremely subtle perfume, and I should like to determine the exact quantity which must be released for you to smell it in every corner of the room. I shall compress this rubber bulb once, and those who detect the fragrance will raise a finger but remain silent. Then I shall repeat the operation until everyone has smelled this perfume." After the first try, there was a heavy silence, a wave of indecision in the audience, and one or two fingers rose timidly. The second time, a few more went up; and, within four or five squeezes, every single finger was raised. The professor then announced, "Gentlemen, there was absolutely nothing in my vaporizer, and you have just wasted a magnificent chance to acquire scientific objectivity."

But there is a second form of servility against which we must warn a child, especially since he is prone to mistake it for independence. I am referring to systematic opposition and the spirit of contradiction—two words that seem to sum up the typical adolescent. Recently, one of our older students here declared, "I was all set to make a good retreat till I found out we *had* to go." "You shouldn't be so sensitive to the mind of your superiors," I answered, "that you'll change your own just because it happens to coincide with theirs." Always saying and doing the opposite of others is not being independent but, rather, depending on them continually. A superior's approbation should not make us abandon our views any more than it should dictate them. Real independence holds to the truth even if our superiors are proclaiming it.

Obstacles

Usually, the biggest obstacle to loyalty is the environment where it has to be practiced. To be loyal when no one else is requires a heroism that few possess. After all, how can one be proud of a flag which everybody laughs at and spits on? In order to make loyalty possible for our children, we must arouse public opinion, shape it and strengthen it, and jolt the good into asserting themselves and uniting.

Start by quizzing your children, at home or at school. You will be astonished at how candidly they reply and how well they state problems which you perhaps did not even suspect. Ask them questions like these: "When do you think it's necessary to lie? In what sort of situations do children lie most often at school and at home? What rules have you decided not to observe as soon as you get a chance? What would you suggest to make parent-child and teacher-pupil relationships franker and more open?"

Their answers will cover every category of prevarication: from the "mythical" lie, which they tell though no one is expected to believe it, to what I call the "sincere" lie, which they tell out of despair because no one would believe the truth. Spend a lot of time with your children discussing the "solidary" or "helpful" lie they use so as not to let a companion down. In the course of these chats, you will perceive that their conscience has to be refined much further; but you will also admire them as you note the simplicity with which they talk about their lies. Furthermore, you will conclude that, in order to keep the ideal of loyalty burning, parents and teachers both must create an atmosphere where this purpose is ceaselessly renewed and intensified by means of discussions, humble avowals, words of encouragement and, principally, by the example of a small but convinced elite.

Inward sincerity must precede outward sincerity. Very often, our children are unfaithful to their obligations or to the rule because they do not know what they want. They are the plaything of contradictory wills, never quite sure which one to follow, always debating, for instance, whether to work or loaf, whether to agree or argue. But it is impossible to taste the joys of concord and the pleasures of conflict simultaneously; impossible, too, to maintain seriously that they are seeking one if they yield their heart to the attractions of the other. Either they must achieve genuine independence by compelling themselves to respect their neighbor's rights, or they must be forcibly recalled to the duties they try to shirk. As it is, they oscillate between insolence and fear, between cowardice and hardihood; and nothing could be more prejudicial to the molding of their personality than all this fluctuation.

Lastly, in the interest of sincerity, we might even ask our youngsters to weigh and counterbalance the exaggerations that are rapidly devaluating contemporary language. Everything is now "super," "fabulous" and "fantastic"; so that when we want to praise someone, we are reduced to saying that he is "really all right."

The Religious Value of Sincerity

There is only one type of person with whom Christ could do nothing: hypocrites. His precepts enjoin poverty, detachment, sincerity, guilelessness and purity of heart, and are totally opposed to the profuse false riches of mendacity.

God demands absolute sincerity. Before him, facades crack and pretenses crumble. He loves us so deeply that we are empowered to renounce self-love; he looks at us with such humility and patience and tenderness that our children and we ourselves are gently persuaded to drop all the masks behind which we anxiously conceal our spiritual barrenness, our inconstancy, our emptiness.

In my mind, there is no greater love than to show someone an image in which he can recognize and accept himself. For the most part, we neither know nor love ourselves; indeed, we hate ourselves and, at any cost, seek a disguise that allows us to cut a figure in the world, protect ourselves from others, and make a favorable impression even through deceit. Just look at our teen-agers: a different pose every week—defiance, stolidity, genius, sophistication—depending on the current best seller or the latest television idol. They play all these roles, weary of them and try still more, without finding their authentic self.

Only the illumination of love can enable someone—by dint of respect and faith in us, of attention, warmth and insight—to make out our true likeness and find a way of revealing it to us. Then, with a mixture of rare humility, of unaccustomed sincerity and joy, we protest, "I don't measure up to your idea of me. It's much too favorable, because you don't know me as I am . . . with all my faults and cover-ups." But, before long, we start to develop a marvelous resemblance to the person he detected in us.

To love others is to call out to them imperiously and to awake, deep in their souls, a mute, hidden creature that cannot help coming forth at the sound of our voice—a creature so new that they did not know him a moment ago, and yet so true that they cannot fail to recognize him now, though they are seeing him for the first time.

God loves us and calls us that way also. His love is always creative, and our truth springs solely from this vocation. Our particular truth is whatever his patient invitations, his tender entreaties and his untiring goodness call us to become. We shall be sincere only when we have evolved into the creature whom God loves, summons forth, nourishes and perpetually raises up within us.

Our truth is to fulfill our calling.

Appendix
FREEDOM*

* Although this essay (*"Liberté"*) was published as a separate book-
let in French, we have included it here as an appendix because of the
light it sheds upon the entire discussion.—Tr.

I FREEDOM AND INDEPENDENCE

Our freedom springs from, and is exercised amid, innumerable dependences. We are as strictly limited at the outset as a pyramid is by its base: the apex may be more or less high and the perpendicular more or less tilted, but the pyramid will never exceed the base from which it rises. We are all involved in a trial by battle. From the start, we are enmeshed in a network of conditions and influences that restrict our freedom even as they give rise to it. We were born without having been consulted; and time, place, family, neighborhood and every circumstance had been determined before we could react. We did not choose to be free, and we are obliged to will even to refuse to will, just as we are obliged to think even to avoid thinking. We can go where we like, but we are forced to leave from where we have been placed.

Yet we instinctively think of our freedom as the absence of all constraint. Passionately, we yearn to do "whatever we please," to select our own course of conduct, our relationships, occupations and leisure-time activities, as we alone see fit. Modern man—and especially modern woman—will brook no limits to self-development. Crushed by duty and law, revolted by tradition and authority, and disturbed by interference and outside influences, we are always on the defensive.

Perhaps there is more skepticism than rebellion in our behavior, more uncertainty than assurance. We no longer believe in anything. Doubt has become the climate of our age; every value has been questioned, every theory contradicted, and every hope deceived. Consequently, we have retired within ourselves as within absolute certainty, fiercely guarding our freedom because we do not dare commit ourselves. Modern man is an unemployed dynamo of generosity. For proof, see how rapturously our contemporaries leap into totalitarian servitude the moment a seemingly good cause promises to lift the burden of freedom off their souls.

121

Today's youths have nothing revolutionary about them (that would presuppose what they lack most: a faith); instead, they are full of goodwill, but mistrustful despite their basic docility, and anarchic because they lack principles and leaders. We may take exception to their very limited goals, but their masters, their experience and the atmosphere they live in hardly allow them to see any further.

With such thin-skinned people, let us proceed cautiously and content ourselves for now with observing what they do when they think they are doing as they please.

1. Opposition

The most childish manner of using one's freedom consists in doing the contrary of what is or was commanded, denying whatever is affirmed, and attempting whatever is forbidden.

Indeed, the worst way to let oneself be dominated is to run counter to an influence and watch it continually in order to contradict it in every detail. Reverse dependence is still dependence; leaning on one's adversary is sheer weakness; and using one's freedom only against others, and never for oneself, is hopeless slavery. The most serious harm our enemies can do is teach us to hate them: they chain us to themselves by forcing us to resemble them. Evangelical charity is a liberating force that breaks the infernal circle in which we once enclosed ourselves. "Love your enemies, do good to those who hate you, bless those who curse you, pray for those who treat you badly." In other words, "Do something different. Emancipate yourselves. Be as independent as your heavenly Father, who causes his sun to rise on bad men as well as good, and his rain to fall on honest and dishonest men alike."

2. Gratuitousness

A second type of person goes further. He is the prisoner, not of other people, but of his own freedom. Insisting that it must always be unhampered and unrestricted, he dreams of exercising it in a vacuum, much as birds might imagine that they could fly more easily without the atmosphere which upholds them but also slows them down.

This man deigns to will only if he cannot give a reason for his acts. Lest he offer a foothold to anyone, including himself, he refuses to formulate his principles; and he even avoids thinking of what he will do next, for fear of being bound by what he has thought. Since he views freedom as absolute spontaneity, as a gratuitous and instantaneous creation, he waits for the impulse that will shape his existence.

Before too long, however, he should notice that this spontaneity is fanned by the merest breath of circumstances, moods and instincts. He has only changed masters. Instead of confronting the old ones and struggling to outwit and overpower them, he has surrendered to all sorts of new ones, invisible but nonetheless real. (Ostriches also are free to believe that their enemy is gone once they have buried their head in the sand. . . .)

Unlimited freedom would be devoid of content, yet the fact is that we all and always want *something*. The person I have been describing, though, wants—and is therefore influenced by—something so poor and fleeting that it goes almost unnoticed. Thus, when his will grasps it, that extremely feeble appeal gives him a sense of power. But this is only a battle of shadows, only a shadow of freedom.

Moreover, he boasts that, by never pinning himself down, he sacrifices none of his potential; and that, by never choosing any one road, he keeps all of them open. On the contrary, he sacrifices everything if he goes through life without knowing commitment, fidelity and love; he definitively blocks off the road to spiritual depth; and he forgoes the most authentic of human experiences— forming and developing oneself through faithful effort. In the end, he will have embarked on every adventure except that of becoming a man.

It is the eternal story of the thousand-dollar bill: too beautiful to spend on any of the things it can buy. Yet, at the close of the day and of life, who is poorer than he who clutches that crisp new bill in his hand—the freedom which has never been put to use?

3. Instinct

Modern man is terribly civilized. All his thoughts, words and deeds are dictated by convention; he lives in a universe of reinforced concrete, of men and women who are just as cerebralized and devitalized as he and just as weary with their lot. Therefore, a potent nostalgia beckons him: "Go back to instinct; be as free as a savage. Send your artificial self packing and unleash the beast in you for once. Let your most animalistic powers take over the direction of your life, so that you needn't think or will any more, but just live at last and feel it all intensely. What a relief it'll be to yield to your instincts, to rely on the dark brute inside you that knows what he likes without having to reflect and gets it without being obliged to will!"

Biological impulses, however, have precise, shortsighted and monotonous goals. They know what they want, but man soon realizes that it is rarely what he wanted (for, like all the weak, he is not sure what he wants but quickly decides what he does not want). Once satisfied, instinct goes to sleep, and leaves him awake; it plunges back into the unconscious in order to recharge itself, and throws him upon his unhappy conscience. It has not liberated him: it has liberated itself but left him shackled to the consequences of its liberation.

4. Lucid Curiosity

In our day, there is still another, more subtle sort of quest for freedom—or, perhaps more accurately, for the impression of freedom. An insatiable curiosity drives contemporary man to indulge in every kind of experience.

He is not afraid of losing his independence meanwhile, because his lucidity, like a periscope riding above his most dangerous descents, guarantees that he shall be in control at all times. Others, for instance, may think they are using him, but he feels sure he is using them twice over. Every temptation duplicates the first one under the tree of the knowledge of good and evil; and, to him, every fall seems fruitful because it is instructive. Similarly, he argues that taking an interest in everything is a way of wanting it all and yet remaining free although he appears dependent.

What with his avidity to know and especially to feel, the most banal and vulgar things can become "interesting." In the immense boredom which characterizes our century, these offer an inexhaustible source of distraction, even if in themselves they seem humiliating and humdrum. All he has to do is give in to his senses, his instincts and whims; then anyone or anything can deliver him from himself for a moment. There is a poetry, a vertigo in this life of abandon where everything is possible and where he waits, ready to be swept along anywhere, since nothing could be worse than remaining alone with the self that he knows too well on the surface and finds too disquieting in depth.

Still, he keeps a certain haughtiness, a certain "dignity" even, thanks to that bitter and disdainfully unavailing lucidity of his. At least, he is no dupe: though his adventures may degrade him, he retains his intellectual freedom and emancipates himself further, even if only from prejudice, fear and ignorance. Awareness of the wrong which he does or suffers gives him the feeling of directing his own life. Even the vilest servitude, he reasons, is not debasing as long as he remains conscious of it; the only evil would be the illusion of freedom, which is unconscious slavery. Provided he can escape that, he gladly renounces reality. But, in point of fact, his lucidity is what creates an illusion of freedom. There is a world of difference between seeing and governing.

Despite his alleged enfranchisement, we detect here again the same debility, the same extreme subjection. Just as a person who lacks the courage to resist an order is incapable of true obedience, so one who never resists an impulse deludes himself into thinking that he remains free because he yields freely. Try as he may to dominate the situation with his critical mind and a keen perception of his master's errors, that vaunted lucidity is only a counterfeit of freedom. He has intelligent views on his bondage, but they do not release him. Liberation would require not only thought but action, which is obviously much more painful.

5. Conclusions

It is not so easy, therefore, to do what we want, for the simple reason that it is not easy to know what we want. Psychoanalysis has taught us a great deal about the hidden motives behind our cleverest rationalizations; and in everyday life, when faced with the consequences of a deed which we vehemently desired, we often echo the words of Kaiser Wilhelm II at the end of World War I: "This I did not want!" I often tell myself that we would be cured of many follies if, for a moment, we could glimpse the sort of person we shall be in twenty years.

Much though we may delude ourselves about our behavior, it never deludes us but ineluctably brings us back to the reality which we were trying to ignore. Paul Bourget entitled one of his novels *Our Deeds Follow Us*. They do. But often they even precede us, dragging us where we do not choose to go. We can rebel against the authority of persons, but we cannot escape the logic of life, which all too frequently shows us that we did not want what we wanted and really wanted what we did not want. Error and falsehood infallibly throw us into chains, whereas the truth will set us free.

When, quite legitimately, someone probes the problem of obedience and duty, the first question to ask him is this: "What are you obeying when you think you're free? Who's actually leading you when you imagine you're going where you please? It's all very fine to be able to disobey laws, but can you disobey your whims?"

Our independence is always relative: we can merely choose which masters we shall serve. Once, during a prolonged strike, the employees were called together to vote on a contract. Most of them wanted a secret vote, so as to enjoy complete freedom; one old workman, however, opposed the idea and demanded a roll-call vote for everyone to hear. "In the polling booth," he explained, "everyone'd be left to his selfishness, his cowardice and his personal or family interests. But in front of his fellow workers, he'll be obliged to think of the common good and vote accordingly. If anything, he'll be freer." Our liberty can be defined as that which makes us better and enables us to justify an action completely.

Since we cannot escape being influenced, we should exercise our freedom by choosing the influences from which we desire to benefit. Furthermore, in order to be ourselves and do what we truly want, we need others, their presence and their support. The mystery of human nature resides in this: that, to be ourselves, we need someone else—but surely not just *any*one else.

The choicest blessing in life is to meet someone who liberates us by teaching us what freedom is, by goading us on to achieve it, and by communicating to us a love for values of which we had an inkling but deemed ourselves unworthy or incapable. Such a person reconciles us with ourselves; and whenever we see him, we regain confidence in our vocation to become free men like him.

Much more than someone to be imitated, a friend, a counselor, a leader is one who helps us to become ourselves again, to know once more what we want, what we love and who we are. He bears witness to the light by giving proof of his freedom.

II THE NATURE OF FREEDOM

Freedom is usually defined as the power to choose, resulting from the indifference of our will toward the values proposed to it.

This notion confuses a symptom with the cause. Indeed, our common experience of freedom consists in the deliberation where, beyond weighing the motives for our decision, we valuate or devaluate them at pleasure. Far from being determined by the reasons we have for acting, we blithely tip the balance in favor of what appeals to us. We want because we want; and we are capable of wanting anything, because it is never the object that makes us will, but we ourselves. Affirming our freedom is a motive that outweighs all others.[1]

[1] I am not saying, like a few existentialists, that we "create" values, but that, quite conscious of our power, we can deny or exalt them as we choose. Sartre's claim that he creates values stems, I believe, from the psychological experience of free determination and from the fact that a value which we have personally discovered always seems to be our own invention. In reality, however, we have created nothing but

But although the act of choosing affords us the strongest sense of being free, it still does not define the nature of freedom.

Let us first observe that freedom, if it lay essentially in choice, would disappear in the act of the will which makes the choice. For, as soon as we will, we no longer choose: we determine ourselves. We would cease to be free, then, the moment we took a decision. There would be freedom only in not willing or in half willing, as when we incline this way and that while pondering a course of action. Choice is but the preface; it disappears in the act. But who would maintain that freedom disappears in a free act?

On the contrary, a little thought will show us that indifference, or hesitancy, is an unfortunate condition of freedom, a sign that the values proposed to us—and, therefore, our commitment to them —are somehow deficient. The fact that we can choose between two goods doubtlessly proves that neither of them determines us; but it also proves that, at bottom, neither of them is suited to us. They leave us indifferent and, therefore, do not permit us to use our faculty of willing to the full.

Does not genuine freedom consist far more in the possibility of adhering with fullest enthusiasm, fullest awareness, and every fiber of our truest self, to a good which activates and liberates our profoundest resources? Then, there is no need to compare this good with others and weigh their respective merits. We are delivered from these miserable details, from all the shilly-shally, and the problem of having too much to choose from.

Thus, we understand that our freedom of choice was but a defect in our freedom of determination. The will is free only if enlightened as to what it really wants, and it fulfills its function as a will in proportion as it can determine itself more completely.

For this reason, we shall never exercise our freedom more fully than in relation to the Being who calls for absolute consent. When both choice and refusal are no longer possible, our capacity to love

---

the new link between that value and ourselves. All of this, which poses as metaphysics, is only psychology—but extremely inadequate: for the mere thought that this creation is purely arbitrary robs it of all interest. If the value which we have discovered is not a real value, ours is certainly not a real discovery.

manifests itself in all its plenitude. At long last, we are free to love infinitely. And instead of crushing us, this transcendent Being, once we have met him, makes us more alive and more truly ourselves than we ever were without him. He alone extricates us from our narrowness, our groping, our errors; he alone, by actualizing all its potential, causes our personality to unfold; he alone is attuned to the intensity of our yearning.

Our freedom lies—or, rather, consists[2]—in this fundamental orientation toward absolute Good. It is that absolute Good which stirs our whole capacity for willing—so much so that we have never wanted anything except because of its connection with, and likeness to, him whom we seek in his works. He alone is desired for himself, and others because of him. In other words, we would never produce an act of the will if we did not implicitly admit the existence of this absolute Good, who alone makes willing worthwhile. If a man were suddenly plunged into total skepticism, not only could he no longer think (or speak, since affirming one's skepticism means contradicting it, and professing one's doubt means being sure of it) but he could no longer will, either, since nothing would be worth the trouble.

Thus, even when we reject God, we do so in virtue of our God-given tendency to want him. This is what Gabriel Marcel expresses so well in *Du refus à l'invocation:* "Who am I to pretend that I do not belong to you? Indeed, belonging to you does not mean that I am your possession, for this mysterious bond does not lie on the plane of ownership, as it would if you were a finite power. Not only are you yourself freedom, but you want and inspire me to be also. You call me to create myself; in fact, you *are* the call. And if I spurn it (that is, spurn you), if I insist that I belong to myself alone, it is just as though I immured myself, just as though I resolved to strangle with my own hands the very reality in whose name I imagine I am resisting you. . . . If this is so, acknowledging that I belong to you is acknowledging that I cannot belong to myself otherwise; even more, it is acknowledging that both belongings are but one and are identical with the only genuine and com-

---

[2] Emmanuel Mounier says, "We are free only if we are not entirely free."

plete freedom to which I can aspire. This freedom is a gift, but I still have to accept it; and the power bestowed on me to accept or refuse it, is inseparable from the gift itself. Furthermore, I can accept my freedom in a way which is tantamount to a refusal; and this refusal, because it bears on the very power which makes it possible, has the earmarks of treason."

Yet this absolute Good remains hidden, to be inferred only from the insatiable drive of our will-as-willing and from vestiges seen in the goodness of creatures. Hence, as long as we remain on earth, we are condemned to choose, never willing as fully as we would wish to, and ceaselessly experiencing this lack, this disproportion between our longing and reality, between what we expected and what we obtain.

Our frustration is so acute that we are perpetually tempted to delude ourselves and lavish infinite love on people and things whom we know imperfectly enough to imagine they are infinite. Such an error of judgment is dangerous for us who give ourselves wholly to objects that can neither receive, vivify nor sustain us. But it is fully as dangerous for those to whom we give ourselves. For our infinite desires, if unsatisfied, ravage and destroy; and, through disappointment at not finding what they seek, they do not appreciate or respect even the little they do find. From wanting the finite infinitely, we soon come to loathe it. Only after we have touched the infinite can we truly and lucidly love beings who, despite their imperfections and limitations, are open to infinity and lead us toward it as soon as we stop making unreasonable demands on them. (As the proverb says, there is no use preaching to a hungry man.) To love someone is to let ourselves be led in the direction which he indicates, and to revere his mystery because we surmise and accept the fact that he is more than he is.

The one corrective for infinitizing the finite is reflection—in other words, measuring a given value against the yardstick of our fundamental appetite for the infinite (or, in more technical terms, comparing the will-as-willed with the will-as-willing). Once we have done so, once we have estimated the indigence of any creature in terms of our absolute avidity, we are *liberated* from that creature because we have sized it up and put it in its place.

We are not free with regard to persons and things until we can judge them; for, as long as they seem to transcend all our categories, they remain indeterminate and therefore appear infinite.[8] This is equivalent to saying that people who do not think are not free. Led by instinct and stirred up by propaganda, the rabble run off in all directions without ever noticing—except later, perhaps—that they did something they did not will to do.

Thus, freedom to choose, and especially freedom to do wrong, is but a weakness of the will, not an essential part of it. "Freedom," wrote Monseigneur de Ségur, "is the power to do what is right, just as judgment is the power to know what is true. The possibility of doing evil has no more connection with the essence of freedom than the possibility of erring has with the essence of judgment, or of falling ill with the essence of health."

Freedom to sin is a pitiful freedom, indeed. Who will make us free enough to stop sinning, to become incapable of sinning, to leave the rest aside and pursue only such goods as we really want?

Now we can understand that the elect love God with the freest and most unshakable act of the will, and that there is nothing unmanning about our obligation to want the absolute and want it always. Freedom means becoming ourselves; it offers us an opportunity for self-development, self-realization. But we attain fulfillment only in giving ourselves, and experience supreme exaltation in loving. Therefore, we are never freer than when we love best. The possession and disposition of self would be an intolerable burden if it did not permit us to be disponible and, as a consequence, liberated from self by effectuating our profoundest impulsion.

To love is to be dependent. Still, no one could reasonably want to shake off this dependence for the horrible freedom of not loving. "As soon as we have gained enough insight into the matter," Gabriel Marcel explains, "we clearly perceive that the opposition

---

[8] Earlier, I remarked that the will, in a manner of speaking, liberates the mind by refusing to bow before the most cogent reasons and imperious motives, since, rightly or wrongly, the will assigns these motives whatever value it wishes. Here I am showing that reflection really liberates the will when the will deceives itself by fashioning an absolute out of what is not.

between autonomy and heteronomy no longer makes sense. I become myself only by consenting, by answering a call which empowers me to answer it."

In our most momentous human experiences, we see the contradiction between law and vital impulse vanish. In the realm of morality, for example, there can be no duty without freedom, but freedom would be meaningless without duty. Or again, love is a free gift, but it is also the most imperative summons for our freedom to devote and consecrate itself. Art, likewise, illustrates this fusion of creative freedom and submission, this uncompromising acceptance of a necessity which the artist heeds passionately, and faithfully obeys.

In fine, we are free only to do our duty. And we are most fortunate if we listen to its call, for it tells us much more about our nature than about our labors.

III   THE PEDAGOGY OF FREEDOM

If freedom is rooted in reflection, and if we must direct our will from what we imagine we want without meaning it toward what we do want without realizing it, then none of us will be free until we free ourselves.

Education is—or should be—essentially that: a begetting unto freedom. However, the whole of modern life conspires against reflection and self-determination. It reduces man to two functions, producing and consuming, and urges him: "Work hard to earn a lot of money, and then spend a lot of money to forget how hard you've worked." Of his taste for freedom nothing remains but a peevish lack of discipline. Too stupefied to know what he wants, the man in the street is too proud to obey; but he proves perfectly docile once the message is aimed at his instincts, his sexuality, his search for the easy way, and his fear of solitude and public opinion.

What our age needs most is to be schooled in reflection, in perspicacious criticism, and independence of judgment and conduct. On that account, education, which until recently always meant the influence of an environment as well as of people, has now become an increasingly specialized endeavor. We must react against our own habits and create a new environment; we must learn to become educators, since the task calls for professionals and leaves no room for amateurs. Only after we have reeducated ourselves can we educate our children.

IV MOLDING THE WILL

Let us define the will briefly as the faculty of accomplishing what we judge to be good. I doubt whether will power can be acquired. Rather, I think we all possess a great deal of it for things we really want, and very little for those we merely say we want. As a matter of fact, the very people who complain of a weak character expend incredible energy resisting everything that would prevent them from weakening.

All of us have vast will power. What we honestly want, we always attain; and a whole-souled desire is infallibly efficacious. God has indeed placed our destiny in our own hands. When a child views the results of an act he performed, he can say, "This isn't what I intended," but we adults have to admit that we are responsible for what we make of ourselves.

"The noble achievements of maturity," as Maurice Barrès used to say, "are always the results of a noble idea we had in our youth." We shall live what we have dreamed of and attain everything we have willed. That is why so many people achieve nothing: they do not know what they want: they want nothing.

With a little faith, Jesus tells us, we can move mountains. But he also warns that there is nothing hidden which will not be revealed, nothing secret which will go unknown; and that whatever we whisper in solitude, on the pillow of our dreams, will be proclaimed from the housetops. And, in truth, the only judgment needed will be our lives. From what we have become, everyone will know what we wanted. Our alleged, unfulfilled intentions will pave the floor of hell, whereas the vault of heaven will scintillate with deeds. A man's real life is not the product of chance: everything that happens to him bears his image and likeness.

Analyze this symptom: Who would want to exchange his lot for someone else's? I do not mean his health, his social standing, his looks, his talents or perhaps his spouse, but his very self, his actual life. Nobody. And those who maintain they would are not thinking; they know neither themselves nor their neighbor. They would like to be him and themselves simultaneously. But just him? Never! If this is true, it proves that all of us are what we wish, that we cling tenaciously to our personality and that, despite our protestations and complaints, nothing would pain us more than changing our mode of being.

Let us not seek to acquire more will power, therefore, but learn to make good use of what we all have. This entails striving for unity and sincerity in our thinking, and transmuting ideas into ideals.

1. Unity and Sincerity

The will is not independent of the intellect. By exerting a certain thrust toward action, every idea in our consciousness triggers a beginning of volition and is thus the start of activity.

Someone with but a single idea would inevitably perform the corresponding act. Take acrophobia and those falls which are described as involuntary but are quite the opposite. If you are a prey to fear of height, you allow yourself to be dominated by that idea till it gradually drives out every other. Then, when all competition has been excluded, the thought that you could fall and are going to fall becomes an irresistible resolution to fall.

Or say you are learning to ride a bicycle, and are not yet sure of yourself and cannot steer straight. The sight of an old man approaching terrifies you as you picture yourself running into him. Well, unless you can conjure up the contrary image and so counterbalance your fear, it will unfailingly materialize; and, although you cannot steer well, you will nevertheless head directly for the old man whom you would have wished to avoid but now *want* to hit.

Nothing is more convincing than to observe this process at the start. To pick one example among many, we all tried, as children, not to step on the cracks in the sidewalk. At first, that was a mere game, played with a blend of calculation and acrobatics; but if we let the idea take hold at all, what had started as a fancy soon became an obligation, an obsession. When we accidentally lighted on a crack, we felt physical discomfort and, even while accompanying our elders, we adopted a grotesque gait lest we violate the taboo.

Any idea that gains possession of us eventually acts itself out. The art of willing, then, consists in focusing on an objective. To will is to persuade ourselves of one idea, and one idea only; to decide is to shut out all others. But to discuss is to weaken.

Here, too, we can learn by watching ourselves practice the art of not willing. Suppose you have set your alarm clock for 6 A.M. So strong is your will that it may very likely keep you insomnious all night, or rouse you repeatedly to check the time, or awaken you at 6 sharp just before the alarm rings.

But let us say you are still sleeping when it goes off. If you offer no resistance and, on awakening, let yourself be ruled by the idea with which you dozed off—"I'll get up at 6"—something surprising and painful will occur: you will get up!

In order to prevent such a catastrophe, you simply deflect your unrelenting will by looking for another idea to liberate you from the first: "Oh, I can take five minutes extra. I'll just hurry a bit more after." When the five minutes have sped by, your original decision returns to offer you a helping hand once more. In a desperate effort to decline it, you have to think up all sorts of other ideas, like "For this morning, I'll wash the quick way" or "I can skip breakfast" or "I'll run to the bus stop"—in brief, anything that excuses you from willing to get up.

For the classic example, watch a schoolboy getting down to his homework. He wants to do it but is depressed at the sheer thought of having to, so that he interposes between himself and his resolve a series of conditions that will give him breathing space. "If I'm going to work right," he rationalizes, "I've got to straighten out my room first. Then open the window. Then draw up a schedule. Then sharpen all my pencils so I won't have to stop once I get going. Then . . ." Then goodness knows what. You see, the poor boy is at his wits' end and has to find some pretext to escape; otherwise, his will—much as he may downgrade it by pleading "I don't have any will power"—is so steadfast and overbearing that it shall promptly put him to work.

Above all else, then, willing is a matter of thinking; but we are always capable of thinking; therefore, we are always capable of willing. The only thing we cannot do is will when our head is teeming with all kinds of thoughts, distractions and objections. We must be sincere with ourselves and not cut off our legs to prove we cannot run.

Over and over again, when speaking to people who insist that they recognize their duty but have a weak character, I have observed that my line of reasoning annoys them. "Quite convincing, quite convincing," they mutter, "no need to go on." Deep down, they dread being talked out of the secret conviction that they are better off not doing their duty. So they go away, declaring and really believing themselves full of goodwill and readiness to discharge their obligations—but still nursing the same illusion.

Indeed, the power of our will is such that, if we did not contravene it by providing loopholes, alibis and distractions for ourselves, we could not escape from it.

If this conclusion is true, it explains why character improvement often comes about suddenly, why a person can change overnight. If the will resembled a muscle which is strengthened by repeated effort, these abrupt transformations would be incomprehensible; but if it is set in motion by convictions, then will power can appear as instantaneously as the convictions themselves.

"I fear the man of one book," said Saint Thomas. No less formidable is the man with one idea, because, sooner or later, he will carry it out. Preferably, this idea should sum up and unify the largest possible complexus of information and reflection. Still, if we are unable to unify the results of our inquiry, we would be wiser to narrow the scope of it than to remain torn between the various directions we have discovered.

2. From Idea to Ideal

There are two kinds of ideas: abstract ideas, which appeal to the intellect but have little influence on behavior—for instance, "It is good to work"; and concrete ideas, which sway the heart—"Oh, it's so nice to do nothing!"

We possess within us a force even greater than the will: our emotions. Only when we love something can we do it well, and our sublimest impulses spring from the heart.

Fortunately, it is possible, through attention and reflection, to change an abstract idea into a concrete one, and thus make it alive and operative. As a consequence, we must use our will, not to act under compulsion, but to make ourselves love our duty.[4] How? Through meditation, where we envision as vividly as possible whatever could render duty attractive. Our ideas have to descend from our head into our heart—and sometimes even down to our toes.

Perhaps a hero is just a man who sees duty as something so stirring that he can easily banish thoughts of fear or self-interest. If he is a genuine hero, he will also be humble because he realizes, firstly, that his exploit was not as difficult for him as it would have been for people with a different set of values; and secondly, that, in domains where he has not forged himself such compelling convictions, he is often as weak as anyone else. I think we could aptly define heroes as men who, in their several spheres, have discovered the joy of doing what is right.

A remarkable person is not one who ceaselessly strains to overcome himself, but one who can convince himself to do his duty gladly. If some new obligation arises, he can promptly call forth ideas that will make it just as sympathetic. The secret is simple: he is in the habit of meditating.

We ought to be humble enough to admit that we cannot act without preparation, without training, without reflection. What we need is to meditate—in other words, to direct our whole attention and energy toward one idea and then impose upon ourselves the interior transformations needed to actualize it. By meditating, we

---

[4] Going against our heart's desire may sometimes be beneficial, since effort can put heart into us and make the same action that frightened us before, not only easier, but often more agreeable than we could ever have suspected. On occasion, therefore, we must either prod or restrain our nature. But unless we do so in order to discover our truer and deeper nature, we shall produce only tension and distaste.

glimpse the sort of men we shall become by doing our duty; whereas by dreaming, which is the direct opposite, we fondly suppose that the metamorphosis has been accomplished and sit back to enjoy the results.

Very few people meditate—which is why very few people are outstanding. Though many would like to act, almost none are willing to hammer out convictions for themselves. A real man is one who loves his duty, while others do theirs grumbling and thinking of something else.

Duty seems so repugnant because we discharge it with divided affections. As has often been said, nothing degrades us like a noble act performed in a mediocre frame of mind. Obeying the voice of duty is not what degrades us, but going through the motions while inwardly resisting, or acting without conviction and through cowardice which is as incapable of love as of rebellion.

At bottom, we do not really will much of what we do in a day. Whenever we can, we cut corners; when we cannot, we drudge under protest. Specifically, we get up only when we cannot stay in bed any longer; we bathe so as not to look too dirty; we leave lest we be unreasonably late; and we do as little as we can get away with. (Yet there is one thing which would be still more disagreeable than working if we were prevented from doing so. . . .)

Having thus exempted ourselves from willing our activity, we lean sullenly on social constraints, like a tired old horse on the shafts of the wagon he should be pulling. This spirit both feeds our resistance and saps our energy; it sends us off to work with our hands tied behind our back. Since we do everything without choosing to, we feel no joy, but only the pressure of obligations and deadlines. In fact, we count on it to whip us into performing duties which we do not exactly want to shake off but are too lazy and cowardly to take on.

A unified man wills what he does; and when asked, "If you could do anything you wanted, what would you choose?" he manifests authentic maturity by answering, "What I'm doing right now." A weak man, on the contrary, dreams of things which he does not truly intend to do, and does things which he never dreamed of. Our dreams should coincide with our duty, so that they may serve as catalysts for it, as motive power and as ornaments to make it appealing.

From this we see the need of filtering the influences which shape our thinking, those we hardly notice and those we deliberately seek out. Every idea that is introduced into our consciousness and cannot be assimilated by our ideal, provokes a hemorrhage of the will, as it were, with consequent anemia. Therefore, we must dream only of what we really want to do, love only friends whom we really want to resemble, and read and see only those books and films by which we want to be inspired. Short of that, we can expect our will to be weak.

At the beginning of this section, I said, "Let us not seek to acquire more will power, but learn to make good use of what we all have." Here I shall suggest how:

1. By setting before us an ideal of self-mastery and, as a start, performing five deliberate acts each day—five acts into which we put our entire will.

2. By planning our conduct, drawing up rules to live by, and keeping a diary (not an outlet for our melancholy, but a witness of our ambitions, a record of our discoveries and a memorial of our best hours). Thus, we shall no longer depend on the flux of events and circumstances, but shall impose our stamp on them.

3. By avoiding means of escape: reveries; idiotic reading matter, which makes no demands on our intellect; the ever-present transistor radio, which accustoms us to not listening; and movies, which train us to neither see nor think. We would benefit far more, in countless ways, if we learned to create our own entertainment. In this connection, may I add that young people especially should not seek pleasures and companionship beyond their age, since a person who likes to feign manliness never achieves it.

4. By not giving in to fatigue or debility too soon. Our morale always collapses before our body. A runner under hypnosis, for example, holds out much longer than one who is awake and imagines he is ready to drop. We can be dead-tired, but if a fire breaks out, not only do we work all night without becoming exhausted but we even feel renewed strength. Almost invariably, we are more fearful than tired. Yet hills flatten out before us when we

start climbing; it is never raining as hard in the street as on our windowpane; and the water is always warmer when we swim in it than when we just dunk our toes.

5. By developing habits that will capitalize the results of our efforts and permit us to enjoy the dividends. Once we have made a decision and embodied it in the corresponding habit, we are free to concentrate on something else. A strong-willed man is not one who perpetually produces acts of volition, but one who can rely on habits that are stable enough to obviate a good deal of hesitating and deliberating.

6. By selecting the kind of friends and environment which incarnate our ideal of life in a dynamic and heartwarming way. "Oh, but my other friends," we think, "are so carefree, so witty, so amusing. They're not the type I'd want to imitate, of course, but I do have such fun when we're together." If we spend enough time with them, however, they will necessarily affect not only our sense of humor but our attitude toward life. Little by little, we shall treat everything as a joke, become irreverent, stop thinking and exerting ourselves, and finally slip into insouciance, that warm blanket where we hide so as not to assume the responsibility for our existence.

Actually, the secret of character training lies far beyond formulas. It rests on total confidence in God and reasonable confidence in self.

Before we can improve, we must accept what we are, take ourselves in hand, and hope mightily. Refusing to accept ourselves is like demanding a radical change which could occur only in a dream and through no effort of ours. With respect and trust in God's generosity, then, let us receive the gift of ourselves from his hands.

There is infinitely more in us than we suspect. Right down to our fingertips, each of us is a unique being, incomparable and irreplaceable. And we can become almost anything we wish, as is obvious from the way we enter into the most diverse mentalities when reading a novel and feel all the characters—the best as well as the worst—live within us.

If only we ply our oars, we shall be amazed at the distance we

cover. If we spread our sails, we need no longer dream of someone offering us a motor. Rather, we should trust that God will
send us a favorable wind to fill them; and when he does, we shall
know that we lack nothing for a happy and confident life.

For this confidence is grounded on God's personal love for each
of us. Our life will make no sense to us unless we come to see it as
a grace from God, a vocation, a call addressed to us by an infinite
Person to love him infinitely in return. Only then will our soul
spread open as it can and aspires to. Only then shall we be able
to draw ourselves up to our full height under heaven—when we
realize that it is peopled by a paternally loving and attentive
Presence.

V FREEDOM AND RELIGION

True religion is essentially liberative. The Redemption is a Pasch,
a passing over from servitude to enfranchisement. "The truth will
make you free. . . . If the Son makes you free, you will be free
indeed." [5] So generous is this freedom that it is cosmic: "Creation
still retains the hope of being freed, like us, from its slavery to
decadence, to enjoy the same freedom and glory as the children of
God." [6]

We shall know, and shall obtain, what we sincerely want. We
shall love one another forever in a world where justice dwells. We
shall be restored to our most natural activity: knowing, loving and
giving thanks. For we are not free, nor do we truly possess our
being, until we offer it to God in a joyous eucharist which raises us
up to him on the same impulsion that carried him down to us.

Yet religion, in point of fact, often spells alienation. Atheists
are not the only determinists: fatalism is the gravest temptation in
any religion, since a certain concept of sacredness enslaves man
to all sorts of fears.

There is a kind of faith in God—bad faith, in the full sense of

[5] Jn. 8, 32.36. (All scriptural quotations are from *The Jerusalem
Bible*.—Tr.)
[6] Rom. 8, 21.

the term—that devirilizes us and makes even true faith in him seem incompatible with faith in mankind. Atheism's chief complaint is that religious people do not do everything they could for the city of man. Through respect or fear of God, and even through laziness, they remain unprogressive and look to him for what they themselves should accomplish. Whatever they cannot explain is "providential"; whatever they cannot do, God will do—as if he exists to compensate our inadequacies. Over against this religion of resignation, of the cross and of failure, there stands contemporary atheism, which has been most perceptively defined as "the rediscovery of human dignity and of man's creative vocation."

Let me briefly outline the basic tenets which many believers profess and unbelievers denounce:

"What can we humans hope to achieve? If God is absolute perfection, there's literally nothing for us to do: initiative and freedom are out of the question.

"God knows everything and foresees everything, so that our fate's already sealed and all we can do is accept it. Like actors on the stage, we play the part we've been cast in but we can't alter the plot.

"Our efforts are futile and leave humanity unchanged. No matter what becomes of us in the next life, God will be glorified: we'll bear witness either to his goodness or to his justice, but we won't have added to them in any way."

Above and beyond these views, there are more subtle alienations, which are not expressed in philosophical language and are not as apparent in everyday life. I shall try to describe them here:

First of all, Catholics are rarely encouraged from the pulpit to esteem and cultivate freedom. In a Church as thoroughly hierarchized as ours, anyone who advocates it becomes suspect. Saint Paul's invectives against the Law are sometimes quoted but obviously restricted to the Mosaic Law instead of being extended to any and all law. Yet "his statements concerning the Mosaic Law, not insofar as it is Mosaic, but insofar as it is law, apply in fact to any law imposed on man from without." [7]

[7] S. Lyonnet, S.J., *Les Epîtres de St. Paul aux Galates et aux Romains,* p. 58.

We admit that the Holy Spirit is a spirit of freedom,[8] but we maintain that the commandments of God and of the Church will always be the foundation of religion. On the contrary, the foundation of religion is the Spirit, who interiorizes these laws in such a way as to make us love them. For a Christian, they are only an apprenticeship in freedom, however long-drawn-out the process may be.

Methodical men, because they distrust liberty and inspiration, are conservatives, whereas the Spirit is inimical to the "old man," to those who have not kept up with the evolution of the world and who stop at the decalogue though we have the beatitudes. Convinced that the status quo is good enough, they do not believe in progressing but only in preserving what they already have. Hence, they store the salt of the earth in the heaviest and most hermetic shakers they can design. Pessimistic about the future and the effectiveness of our activity, they believe that sin will always triumph and that this world will be destroyed in some ultimate cataclysm. Accordingly, they do very little to better it. None of this either evinces or fosters freedom.

That is why a certain brand of atheism can unquestionably virilize us. Before we can embrace the true religion, we must renounce our false one. But let us never forget that atheism ennobles us only because of the vestiges of Christianity which it contains: faith in life and in mankind, the hope of salvation, and human brotherhood. In itself, if it were logical, it would dehumanize man utterly, since everything is allowed if God does not exist. Unfortunately, this is the kind of atheism—still more cowardly and passive than the worst of religions—which most young men espouse when they lose their faith.

1. God and Human Freedom

God is free and wanted us to be free, with a freedom so complete that he made us capable of disobeying him, and a freedom so broad that he made us responsible for our brothers and the entire world.

[8] 2 Cor. 3, 17: "Where the Spirit of the Lord is, there is freedom."

Though veiled, the Absolute exists and manifests himself to us discreetly through creation, which he invites us to understand and perfect, and through the revelation which he proposes to us. The infinite not only tolerates the finite but creates it, maintains it in existence, and wants it to live outside of him and evolve according to the resources with which he has endowed it.

God does not "foresee" what we are going to do. By saying so, we place him in time. He knows his creatures as they are: the free ones as free, and the determined ones as determined. His knowledge follows upon their nature and does not change it. "St. Thomas explains that 'the *first cause* of a lack of grace comes from ourselves,' *defectus gratiae causa prima est ex nobis*. . . . In the line of evil-doing, it is the creature that is the first cause. . . . If the creature has indeed the first initiative in the line of evil, it thereby—negatively—intervenes in the very moulding of the designs of providence. In that eternal moment, in which all the moments of time are held, God, if one may say so, in making and seeing in one single glance the whole of human history, waits on each one of us, on our refusal or acceptance of the gifts of that sovereign power from which all being and all action derive—all things, save the nothing we may bring." [9]

In creating us free, God wished to limit himself. (To quote Gabriel Marcel, "I am free insofar as God sets bounds to his productive power.") It is not we who limit his omnipotence; it is he who has chosen to reveal it in an infinitely more beautiful way by creating creators, by giving his creatures something to give him in return—and something with which to resist him.

Thus, through the institution of the Church, God has willed to need men. Our collaboration in the Redemption is indispensable. Instead of dimming God's power, this truth makes it shine forth. Is it not far worthier of him to have enabled us to give rather than merely receive?

God will never force us to love him. He does not just make believe that he is soliciting our consent, but has really left us both

[9] Jacques Maritain: *True Humanism,* tr. by Margot Adamson (New York: Charles Scribner's Sons, 1938), pp. 68–69.

initiative and responsibility. Even the angels were able to refuse.

And still, God remains the great Lord of history—not like a dictator, but like a love that abides however often we may spurn and betray it. Rather than a composer directing a performance of his own works, he is an improviser who, at each moment, invents something to blend with what he has just heard, making it all fit into and serve his creation.

God permitted the terrifying risk entailed in human freedom only because he knew that his love can outmaneuver whatever we may do to spoil our lives. A solemn dialogue was inaugurated between God and us. We act as we please, but he always finds some way to triumph over the evil we do. From each of our faults he gives us the power to make a "happy fault." Thus he restores even more admirably than he first created. Much more than of our woes, original sin is the origin of the marvels that God has devised to repair it. Adam was replaced by Christ; and Eve by Mary, the mother of the living. Let us be confident, then: he will overcome evil, he already has overcome it. If we are dead, he will raise us up. God's superiority rests on his indefectible fidelity, on his new and eternal covenant: never will he give up the idea of loving us and saving us. We, on the other hand, are fickle even in our fickleness, yet this very inconstancy is an ever-open door to God's tender patience. But he can be vanquished, because he has willed so.

Beyond a doubt, all the good we do comes from God—but from God, too, comes freedom and responsibility for our deeds. His grace is not what some earlier theologians described as a "motion," but a call which makes us capable of answering.

2. Christ and Freedom

Christ is our Deliverer. Christianity means faith in a Power of liberation which makes us pass from the world of bondage to the Kingdom of Freedom.

Being men, we are enslaved to innumerable masters: to our blindness, our passions, our fellowmen, our sins, and death. Law has no liberative force. A mere signpost, it gives useful information but does not carry us one step forward. The risen Christ is the only man who is free and who frees us.

The Redemption is the process of manumitting the world by warring against its servitudes—sin, with all its personal, social and cosmic consequences. Therefore, we must not think in terms of spiritual liberation only, for there can be no such thing without political, social, economic and technological liberation as well. The Gospel and the transformation of human structures are linked by mutual causality.

As Christians, we know that we are responsible for the salvation of the world and should not consider ourselves freedmen as long as one solitary person remains a slave. Our goal is not to escape from the world but to welcome, into its life as well as ours, this power of total liberation which is Christ.

The Church constitutes an atmosphere of holy freedom—that is to say, of genuine charity. By casting off outworn forms in every age, she preserves purity of spirit and inspires the societies around her to do likewise.

Her laws are not handcuffs but keys to emancipation. If we regard them only as "commandments" and observe them without love, we do exactly like the Pharisees who condemned Christ in the name of their Law.

Sad to say, many Christians shift their responsibility to think and will onto the Church. Thanks to this dodge, one can live the most pusillanimous life in the noblest religion of all. The Church demands obedience, of course, but filial obedience. We know that in obeying our lawful superiors, within the limits of their competency, we are obeying Christ, who enjoins us to hear them as we would hear him. Theirs is the duty of making sure that, when they command, he is commanding through them.

The filial role of the faithful consists in helping their ecclesiastical superiors—by means of intelligent, alert, active obedience—to be the spokesmen for none but Christ. Essentially, passive obedience is passive resistance. Obeying never excuses anyone from acting and thinking. Too many Christians behave toward the Church like shareholders in a joint-stock company: they receive dividends but show no deeper interest in its workings. This is culpable abdication.

The worst service laymen can render to authority is a timid submissiveness that encourages authoritarianism. To some extent, the clericalism which so many denounce today is the inevitable consequence of passiveness on the part of the laity. We are all responsible in the Church, though in different capacities, ways and degrees. The Church makes us, but we also make the Church. Therefore, we ought to think, search and cooperate actively with those in authority, express our views, furnish information and even submit our objections. Obedience to the Church is a duty of conscience, not an invitation to inconscience.

If the Church in this century has lost the allegiance of the multitude and if she often seems behindhand and irrelevant, that is because she has not been made present to our contemporaries by those millions of routine Christians who live as people have always lived or—to put it still more simply—who live like everybody else, instead of feeling collectively responsible for the incarnation of Christ in today's world.

But if we enthusiastically shoulder this responsibility, we practice a religion which virilizes and liberates us, a religion which fulfills Christ's promise: "If you make my word your home, you will indeed be my disciples; you will learn the truth, and the truth will make you free. . . . I tell you most solemnly, everyone who commits sin is a slave. . . . If God were your Father, you would love me. . . . [The devil] is a liar, and the father of lies. . . . A child of God listens to the words of God; if you refuse to listen, it is because you are not God's children." [10]

"If you make my word your home, you will indeed be my disciples." We have to live in it and by it—not remaining passive, mute or crushed, but loving it, pondering and putting it into practice. Jesus incites us to activate our faith.

"You will learn the truth, and the truth will make you free." Like the Pharisees, we are unconsciously steeped in falsehood. First of all, there are the lies which we tell as individuals and which warp our own nature. For when we lie, we lie to ourselves first; and when we lie to ourselves, we wander into an impasse, we become lost in an unreal world where everything we do drags us in

[10] Jn. 8, 31–32.34.42.44.47.

still further. We pretend that we do not like what we are doing. Yet, when urged to stop, we protest, "No, I can't; I simply don't have the courage it takes," whereas we should frankly admit, "I don't want to." Conversely, we pretend that we love the things we do not do. Yet, when urged to start, we again protest, "No, I can't; I simply don't have the courage that takes, either." We want and do not want. So badly has falsehood disfigured us that we do not know who we are or what we really desire. Secondly, and especially, there are the lies which we tell as a body: the lies of a world that calls itself Christian or just or civilized, but is not; the lies of an elite who imagine they are offering leadership but, actually, are seeking only to dominate and possess; and the lies of groups which have capitulated to money, pleasure, sex, sloth or public opinion. Again, we do not recognize ourselves and are content merely to play a role.

"I tell you most solemnly, everyone who commits sin is a slave." And this slavery is as horrible as it is multiform. Never very funny, even in itself, sin sets off a terrifying chain reaction—evil companions, illicit relationships, habits, disgust, blindness, paralysis of the will, and finally despair. Still, we tell ourselves that we are free! If only we could become aware of our servitude on all levels, we would also become capable of deliverance. Let us, then, cry out to Jesus, our liberator, for his words will produce this awareness and effect this deliverance once we allow him to reveal us to ourselves, to challenge and criticize us. "If the Son makes you free, you will be free indeed."

"If God were your Father, you would love me." We would sense that Christ is calling us to be free, to grow, to become loving and proud sons once again. When we listen to his words, God moves and works within us, but we refuse to surrender to him.

"Because [the devil] is a liar, and the father of lies." We are Christians but do not do the works of Christ; we pretend we love, but will not commit ourselves; we pretend we believe, but have no faith. Deep within the religion of Truth, the devil has insinuated his lies.

But "a child of God listens to the words of God." If we refuse to listen, it is because we are not God's children.